THE PICTORIAL
ENCYCLOPEDIA OF
BIRDS
OF THE WORLD

THE PICTORIAL ENCYCLOPEDIA OF
BIRDS
OF THE WORLD

MARK RAUZON

GALLERY BOOKS
An imprint of W.H. Smith Publishers Inc.
112 Madison Avenue
New York, New York 10016

Published by Gallery Books
A Division of W H Smith Publishers Inc
112 Madison Avenue
New York, NY 10016

Produced by
Brompton Books Corp
15 Sherwood Place
Greenwich, CT 06830

ISBN 0-8317-6911-4

Printed in Spain

10 9 8 7 6 5 4 3 2 1

Page 1: The American Bittern relies on camou-
flage when danger threatens, freezing into a
reed-like pose with body, neck, and bill
pointed skyward.

Page 2: A relative of the kingfishers, the
Carmine Bee-eater is among the most attractive Old World birds.

These pages: The Common Crane breeds
widely across northern Eurasia and winters in
Africa. They are inhabitants of open marshlands, wet plains, and prairies.

Edited by Timothy Jacobs

Designed by Tom Debolski

CONTENTS

INTRODUCTION

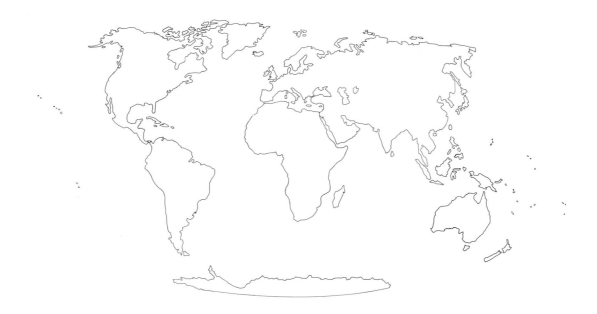

The world of birds is a colorful kingdom populated with more than 8600 species existing in virtually every habitat on the face of the Earth. The resplendent spectrum of color, iridescence and filamentous finery is a miracle to behold. The vocal repertoire of songsters pouring out their song is astounding, and the range of behaviors accompanying this couturial and auditory display sets birds far apart from other animal species, and places them in a realm of beauty they alone inhabit.

Hundreds of millions of birds flee the northern cold, passing on ancient paths called flyways. Major flyways in the world connect Europe to Africa, Asia to Australia and North America to South America. Bird navigation continues to astound and mystify scientists. Birds are able to orient their position relative to the sun and stars. In order to use the sun for navigation, they must have a sense of *time* as well. Some birds have 'compasses' in their brains — tiny crystals of magnetite that respond to the Earth's magnetic fields.

The most spectacular example of migratory capability is that provided by the Arctic Tern, which, breeding above the Arctic Circle in perpetual sunlight, embarks on a flight over the trackless ocean to the limits of the Antarctic ice pack and returns the following spring to the place it left — a yearly flight of over 20,000 miles!

Living in geographical contexts beyond political boundaries, birds are citizens of biogeographic regions, which are, roughly, based on the various major continents or combination of continents on which they live. The largest of these regions is Eurasia, which contains the Arctic and Temperate areas of the Old World. The African and South Asian biogeographic regions are composed of the Tropics of the Old World. North America embraces the Arctic and Temperate zones of the New World, while South America is the Tropics of the New World.

Australasia includes Australia and the adjacent islands of New Zealand and New Guinea. Oceania includes the scattered islands and atolls of the vast Pacific Ocean, and Antarctica includes the polar islands and 'the frozen continent' itself. Both Oceania and Antarctica are considered sub-regions of Australasia.

The history of mankind's fascination with birds is both ancient and modern. Flying birds have long fueled man's imagination, and have kindled his spirit to soar — to take his first flight at Kitty Hawk and ride the *Eagle* to the moon. However, for as much as humans have respected most species through the years, we have made it impossible for some species to survive. To make it possible for us to continue to admire and enjoy these feathered creatures with whom we share the planet, it is useful to know them and to understand the vast profusion of species. Such is our hope with this book.

At left: **A male Common Peafowl, a native of southern India and Ceylon.** *At right:* **A juvenile Red-tailed Hawk.**

EURASIA

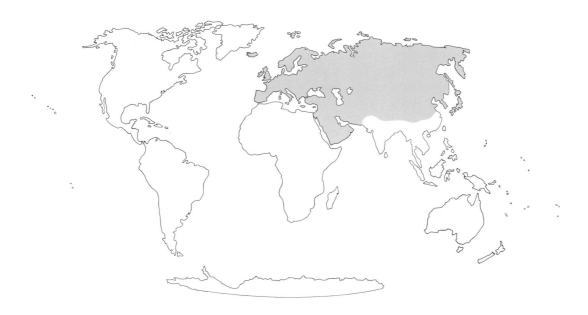

Europe and northern Asia constitute the northern portion of the Old World. From the Atlantic coast of the British Isles to the Pacific coast of Siberia and from the Arctic Ocean to the Mediterranean Sea, Eurasia spans approximately 7000 miles east to west and 4000 miles north to south. Each climatic zone in this vast area supports approximately 1500 distinct species of birds. However, the number is small compared to the tropical regions. The frozen tundra of the far north is devoid of all but a handful of species in the winter. But in summer, the thawed tundra becomes a nesting ground for tens of millions of plovers, redshanks, stints, geese and other water birds. The water-soaked sponge of mosses, grasses and shrubs provides myriad insects and berries in a fertile, albeit temporary, burst of productivity in the constant summer daylight.

The evergreen and birch forests spanning the northern latitudes are inhabited by finches, woodpeckers, grouse and birds of prey that are adapted to harsh winters and reside in the northern woods year-round. The broadleaf deciduous forests of the temperate latitudes support many species like jays, magpies, crows, tits, robins and warblers. The riverine forests bordering watercourses have been severely affected, especially where man has cultivated extensively. The broad steppes, or grasslands, of the Eurasia interior have been converted to farm and grazing land. Grain-bearing crops have replaced native grasslands for the most part. Birds such as crows, starlings and sparrows, which have adapted to manmade changes, prosper with abundant grain and human garbage to eat. However, the overall variety has decreased in favor of fewer species with greater populations.

Europe merges into Asia at the Ural Mountains, located in the Soviet Union. Aside from these mountains, which run north to south, the prevailing Eurasian mountain ranges run east to west, replicating the north to south climatic zones. From the icy alpine fields to the fir-clad slopes, from the broadleaf lowlands to the grassland plateaus, the entire sweep of north to south climates is represented in vertical relief and allows bird species to inhabit a variety of habitats within a relatively short distance.

The Pyrenees Mountains of Spain and France are a hazard for migrating birds because a significant percentage of them are shot by sport hunters. More than one-quarter of the European birds, one million birds of 100 species, cross these mountain passes rather than fly over the Mediterranean Sea. The majority of the birds migrate to the warmer climes of Africa. The southern continent of the Old World serves as a wintering ground until the harsh weather passes and the birds return north once again.

The rocky coastlines of the north are bathed in cold water rich in

At left: A Little Egret of southern Eurasia. At right: A Bohemian Waxwing (top) and a Eurasian Moorhen (below).

marine life. Here vast seafowl rookeries flourish. **Thick-billed Murres** *(opposite, top left)* are the northern counterparts of the Penguins of the Southern Hemisphere. Unlike Penguins, Murres can fly and inhabit vertical sea cliffs in large numbers. They build no nest but lay an elliptically shaped egg on a rocky ledge. The egg spins in a tight circle, which prevents it from rolling and falling off the precarious nest site.

Sharing the cliff are **Kittiwakes** *(opposite, top right),* which plaster their seaweed nests to narrow rock ledges with guano. Several eggs are laid, but the number of nestlings fledged is highly dependent on the food available in nearby waters. Kittiwakes are named after their peculiar cry and are distinguished from other gulls in the northern oceans by a black 'dipped in ink' mark on their wingtips.

The ghost-white **Glaucous Gull** *(right)* is a predator and scavenger of the coastline. It courses on updrafts above the sea bird colonies, always on the lookout for eggs and chicks from unattended nests to eat. **Audouin's Gull** *(below)* is one of the rarest gulls in the world. Fewer than 1000 remain to breed on isolated islands in the Mediterranean Sea. It feeds over deep water and winters in the Atlantic Ocean off northern Africa.

Common Eiders *(opposite, bottom)* are heavy-bodied sea ducks that dive for mollusks and crabs. The female plucks downy feathers from her breast to line a grass nest. The feather down keeps the eggs warm, especially in the cold, damp climate of rocky islands in the far north. The down is collected from the nests by villagers who make pillows and jackets of superior quality.

Black Terns *(below)* inhabit freshwater marshes and lakes, where they build a nest of floating vegetation and lay two or three eggs. The young are fed insects caught on the wing and small fish caught by plunging into the water. Black Terns molt their breeding dress and assume a mottled black and white appearance in winter.

Whiskered Terns *(opposite, bottom)* are also denizens of the freshwater marshes. Found across Eurasia and into Australasia, they build a floating nest and feed by snatching small fish just below the water's surface. **Sandwich Terns** nest in dense colonies on sandbars isolated from predators along the coasts of Europe and North America. One or two chicks are reared on a diet of fish and crustacea procured by diving, often entirely underwater.

The **Pratincole** *(opposite, top right)* is a strange shore bird that looks like a cross between a tern and a plover. With short, tern-like legs, long wings and a forked tail, the Pratincole hunts over grasslands near shallow water for flying insects, which are taken with a stubby, plover-like bill. Pratincoles occur throughout warm regions of the Old World.

The **Lapwing** *(opposite, top left)* is a crested plover typical of European farming country. It is commonly found around farm fields, mud flats, marshes and sewage treatment plants, where it runs haltingly and picks up insects and snails. This wary bird is difficult to approach.

Black and white **Avocets** *(right)* are shore birds that frequent shallow waters, skimming small mollusks and crustacea from the

mud with their scythe-like bills. The **Black-tailed Godwit** *(opposite, bottom right)* probes the mud deeply with its upturned bill for invertebrates such as marine worms and crustacea. Large shore birds with long legs and bills hunt in deeper water than smaller shore birds. **Little Stints** *(opposite, top right)* are the smallest European waders. They are usually seen with others of their own species scurrying along the margins of lakes, picking up minute crustacea from the shore. **Spotted Redshanks,** *(opposite, top left)* while distinctively colored in the summer, trade their black plumage for gray in the winter. Their legs, however, remain red year-round.

The smallest diving birds in Eurasia are **Little Grebes**, petite birds of lakes, ponds and coasts. The slightly larger **Black-necked Grebes** *(right)* inhabit the same types of waters. Their legs are placed so far back on their bodies that walking is very difficult, so they rarely venture on land. Instead, they build a nest of floating vegetation and feed on aquatic invertebrates and fish.

With their graceful, curved necks, arched wings and orange and black bills, **Mute Swans** *(below)* are the picture of peace. Weighing up to 30 lb and with a six-foot wingspan, the fiercely protective swans will hiss at and bite anything that gets close to their nests. Swans, who mate for life, construct a nest of grasses at the edge of the marsh. After 35 days of incubation, the young cygnets hatch and soon strike out on the water with their protective parents. These large water birds have been introduced to, and have established wild populations in, North America and elsewhere.

14

Tufted Ducks *(right)* are common in freshwater marshes across Europe and Asia, occasionally reaching North America. Tufted Ducks occur in large flocks in winter with the similar-appearing **Scaups** and other diving ducks that feed on aquatic animal and plant matter. Only the males have the characteristic tufts on the backs of their heads.

Kingfishers *(opposite, top left)* are common in summer around freshwater marshes and in winter in tidal pools, where they plunge headfirst into the water to seize fish. They also dig tunnels into stream banks and steep cliffs, where they lay their eggs. The young are fed until they fledge. Then the parents may begin nesting again and produce another brood in the same season.

Grey Herons *(below)* are found across Eurasia and into Australia, and appear very similar to the Great Blue Heron of North America. These tall, slender birds hunt aquatic organisms by standing motionless until prey is sighted. Instantaneously, their dagger-like bills impale the prey. Grey Herons may nest on tree colonies with **Purple Herons** *(opposite, bottom)*, a slightly smaller species that has longer toes and is more likely to take prey from floating vegetation.

The very rare **Hermit Ibis** *(opposite, top right)* was bred in Europe until the sixteenth and seventeenth centuries. As a result of its specialized nesting requirements, the species is in grave danger of extinction. Unusual for an ibis, it prefers cliffs for nesting and rather dry areas for foraging. Agricultural irrigation has expanded into its habitat and pesticide pollution and human encroachment have its

16

number down to 200 pairs that breed in Turkey and Morocco. The related **Sacred Ibis** was venerated by ancient Egyptians as a manifestation of Thoth, god of wisdom and learning. Over 1.5 million Sacred Ibis mummies were found entombed, indicating the species was raised commercially and sold to devotees of Thoth.

White Storks have flourished in Europe where other birds have not because storks are considered harbingers of luck and bearers of babies. White storks commonly nest atop roofs and chimneys, often on platforms specially built to accommodate them. In the winter, they migrate to Africa. Flying high in large flocks, they are sometimes victims of hailstorms. They eat grasshoppers, rodents and other invertebrates.

Black Storks *(below)* have not fared as well as White Storks, perhaps because these shy birds are wary of humans. Consequently, their population in Europe has dwindled, but another population has begun nesting in South Africa. The Eurasian birds also migrate to Africa to escape harsh winters. They eat tadpoles, frogs and fish and breed on marsh vegetation and favored cliff ledges year after year.

Flocks of **Eastern White Pelicans** *(right and opposite)* inhabit the lakes and marshes of Europe, nesting in colonies on islands free from predators. They also hunt together as a swimming flock by herding fish into the shallows and then repeatedly diving to catch fish in their capacious pouches. When fully expanded, a pouch holds several gallons of water. The pelicans drain off the water before swallowing the fish. With large black and white wings, these pelicans are among

the largest flying birds in Eurasia — their size being a factor which emphasizes the comic demeanor of these ungainly birds.

Imperial Eagles *(right)* breed in the remote regions of Spain, and from southeastern Europe to central Asia. Some populations migrate to Africa in winter. These large, heavy birds build massive nests in isolated, all trees on the steppes and plains. Despite their slightly smaller size, they are confused with Golden Eagles but differ in having white feathers on their backs.

Steppe Eagles *(opposite, top)* spend a lot of time on the ground, even nesting on the ground in the grasslands of Eurasia and Africa, where they eat birds, rodents, flying termites and carrion. Northern populations are migratory and winter in Africa.

Goshawks *(opposite, bottom)* are rather rare hunters of the northern woods. Female Goshawks are much larger than males, a characteristic shared by many birds of prey. Their long tails and broad wings are designed for maneuverability. Powerful Goshawks fly with great agility through trees and branches, hunting large birds such as jays and grouse.

Saker Falcons *(below)* inhabit the steppes of central Asia, where they nest on rock ledges and cliffs. No nest is constructed: eggs are laid directly on the ground. Saker Falcons hunt by hovering above their prey, then dropping on the unsuspecting animals, which range in size from insects to ducks. They are used for falconry and are also mistakenly shot as vermin by the ignorant.

Immature **Red-footed Falcons** (below) resemble young **Hobbys** — small insectivorous hawks of Europe. When fully grown, Red-footed Falcons are handsome but smallish falcons, with long, tapering wings designed for speed. Gregarious by nature, they may be seen in flocks of 100 in eastern Europe, where they hunt grasshoppers, flying insects and small mammals. Males greatly outnumber females.

Black-shouldered Kites are found across Eurasia and Africa, roosting and breeding socially in small groups. Kites are recognized by their characteristic hovering while scanning the ground for prey. Where numerous, Kites gather to feed on dead animals and rodents and are welcomed by farmers as pest controllers.

The **Eagle Owl** (right) is the grandest predator in Eurasia. More powerful than its namesake, this owl is known to take insects, reptiles, birds and even small deer as food. The Eagle Owl is intolerant of other birds of prey in its territory and will even kill eagles with its lethal talons and the vise-like grip of its feet.

A ghostly resident of the northern evergreen forest, the **Great Grey Owl** (opposite) has a characteristic rounded head and face that is renowned for its noble lines. Flattened facial discs direct sound to the owl's sensitive ears. The owl has velvet-covered feathers, enabling it to fly soundlessly. Rustling feathers would alert its prey, as well as distract the owl itself. On muffled wings, this owl hunts medium-sized rodents at night.

Tawny Owls *(right)* with liquid brown eyes and mottled brown plumage are a smaller version of the Great Grey Owl, hunting small rodents, insects and worms. Owls do not digest the bones and fur of their prey but instead regurgitate 'pellets.' A good way to locate their daytime roosts is to locate the grey pellet piles.

Long-eared Owls *(below)* inhabit evergreen and broadleaf forests near parks and cultivated land. They compress their bodies and appear to be part of the trees they roost in during daylight hours. After dark, they sweep across fields searching for small rodents to eat. **Little Owls** *(opposite, top)* are very adaptable. They are equally at home nesting in rabbit burrows or tree holes. They become most active at dusk, when they hunt beetles and small animals, but may be seen during the day 'bobbing' when agitated.

Nightjars *(opposite, bottom)* are owl-like creatures. Their cryptic coloration effectively hides them as they sleep during the day on tree limbs. At dusk, they fly over the fields and forest clearings hunting moths and other aerial insects. Nightjars have unusually large mouths surrounded by stiff bristles, a tactile feature which makes hunting at night a bit easier. Folklore erroneously credited these birds with sucking milk from goats.

Willow Grouse subsist on buds and seeds from the shrubby willows that grow in the far north. These grouse turn white in winter to match their snowy surroundings. They even develop feathering on their toes to aid in walking on snow.

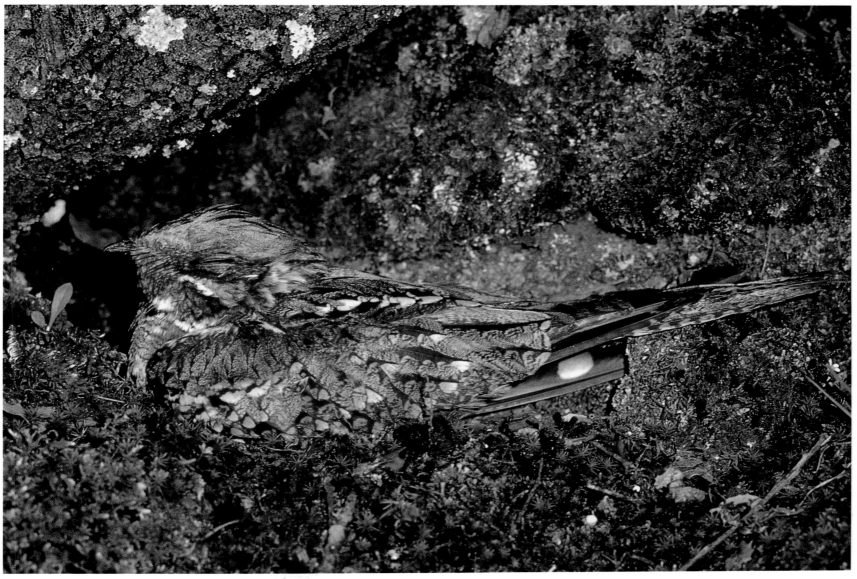

The **Capercaillie** *(below)* of the northern coniferous forest is the largest species of grouse, weighing up to 13 pounds. Its turkey-sized body conserves heat during the frigid winter because larger bodies lose heat less quickly than do smaller ones. It is one of the few birds to eat the conifer needles. In winter, it enters deciduous forests to search for buds and nuts.

Breaking into erratic flight when flushed, the **Grey Partridge** *(right)* is a much sought-after game bird. Coveys winter together, eating leftover grain in the agricultural fields and grasslands. In summer, this bird eats ants and other insects. A well-fed female will lay up to 20 eggs in one nest, and the eggs are tended by both parents. The partridge population is decreasing because of pesticide poisoning and loss of agricultural land to development.

Great Bustards *(opposite)* are very large terrestrial birds of the Eurasian steppes. Foraging in the grasslands and cultivated grain fields, they eat small mammals, insects, seeds and buds. They themselves are hunted for meat and sport, particularly by falconers who like to fly their Goshawks against them. Consequently, Great Bustards are quite rare. They are well known for their amazing breeding displays, during which they appear to turn themselves almost inside out. The male birds throw their wings back and tilt forward, exposing masses of white feathers.

Red-rumped Swallows *(opposite, top)* are common summer residents over most of the Northern Hemisphere. They are great insect eaters and very beneficial to farmers. Vacationers also benefit, since a high portion of the swallows' food is mosquitoes. Humans have repaid the debt many times over, however, because Red-rumped Swallows usually build their mud nests under roofs or eaves. It's hard to imagine where the birds placed their nests before using manmade structures!

Crag Martins *(right)* build nests with mouthfuls of mud and place their nests under granite ledges, cliff faces, in caves or any dry areas in the mountainous regions of Eurasia. They often hunt with other swallows and swifts for aerial insects on the wing.

Azure-winged Magpies *(opposite, bottom)* have two distinct populations that are isolated in Spain, and Korea and Japan. In these areas, they inhabit broadleaf forests, parks and suburbs, usually in small but noisy and aggressive flocks. Pairs become secretive when nesting, trying to evade the parasitic cuckoo.

The **Great Spotted Cuckoos** *(below)* has evolved parasitic breeding behaviors that take advantage of other birds. The female Cuckoo finds the nest of a large bird, such as a magpie, and waits until the female lays her first egg. The Cuckoo then removes the magpie egg and replaces it with one of her own. The female magpie then incubates and rears the Cuckoo chick. A Cuckoo will place several eggs in foster nests each season.

The **Syrian Woodpeckers** *(opposite, bottom)* are expanding their range from the Middle East into temperate Europe. Open woodlands near towns are preferred habitats. Pairs drill a nest in a dead tree and lay several white eggs. They use the hole for several years, then abandon it and dig a new one. Old nests are quickly reoccupied by other hole-nesting birds.

European Rollers *(opposite, top)* rear four or five young each year in tree holes abandoned by woodpeckers. Rollers are named for their tumbling acrobatic maneuvers during breeding. The colorful birds perch on telephone poles and wires, looking for locusts, grasshoppers and dragonflies. When food is spied, they drop down to pounce on their prey. Northern populations migrate to the African savannas in winter.

European Bee-eaters *(below)* also are found in open country, where they perch on telephone wires. Colorful and conspicuous, they careen swallow-like to pluck wasps and bees from the air. Like other bee-eater species, they dig six-foot tunnel nests into sandy banks with their feeble feet.

Starlings *(right)* are familiar to country and city dwellers alike because these stocky, glossy-plumaged birds forage in pastures as well as city parks. Very adaptive to the human environment, starlings have spread across Eurasia and North America, where they nest in cliff and tree holes, as well as under eaves and roofs. During the winter, starling flocks reach pest proportions. They roost nightly in favored trees and defecate profusely. On the positive side, starlings do eat great quantities of insects.

Another pest species is the **Rock Dove** *(right and below)*. There are many genetic variations of the Rock Dove, including carrier pigeons and fancy show varieties. So successful are these birds that they have spread virtually around the world. Cities provide habitats that are similar to the sea cliffs, mountain faces and other stony areas where they originally nested.

The **Great Tit** *(opposite, higher bird)* is the largest, most common and wide ranging of the titmice family in Eurasia. Its range is from the British isles to the Indonesian islands. They are a favorite at bird feeders because they eat seeds, fruit and caterpillars.

The **Blue Tit** *(opposite, lower bird)* has only a slightly smaller range. Both species are regarded as relatively intelligent compared to other birds. The Blue Tit is notorious for having learned to drink milk by piercing the seal of the bottle. This behavior soon spread widely across the English countryside among birds of the same species.

The **Bearded Tit** is a resident of extensive reed beds in Britain, northern Europe and Asia. It climbs reed stalks, jerking its long, loose tail. Its whirring flight is unique. The nest is placed low among the reeds by the male and tended by the female. Two or more broods a year may be reared on small insects and seeds.

European Robins *(right)* are confiding birds and will often approach humans, perhaps because humans often flush insects out of hiding and into the robin's view. Berries and fruit are eaten in fall. In years with good food crops, three broods may be reared. A nest of dry leaves and feathers is hidden under ivy or in the undergrowth in gardens, parks, broadleaf forests and conifer woodlands. Each nest holds five to seven bluish-white eggs speckled with red.

Bluethroats *(opposite, top)*, like robins, are ground-loving species fond of snails and insects. But unlike robins, they are more secretive and difficult to spot. Bluethroats inhabit brushy streamside vegetation in which the male builds a nest of fine grasses and rootlets. If all goes well, within a month up to seven young may leave the nest. Partial to colder climates, Bluethroats are found across northern Eurasia. A population has crossed the Bering Straits and now inhabits Alaska. In the winter, they migrate to northern Africa.

The **Stone Chat** *(below)* is also found in drier habitats, nesting on the ground in low branches and moist grasses along streams across Eurasia and Africa. This generally silent bird eats such insects as dragonflies and flying termites.

Yellow Wagtails *(opposite, bottom)* walk across the wet ground, picking up insects as they constantly pump their tails up and down. Wagtails breed in moors and marshes across Eurasia, extending their

range into coastal Alaska. Migrating into Africa and south Asia, they inhabit rice paddies and other agricultural land in winter.

Finches are seed-eating birds with bills especially suited to their individual diets. The massive bill of the **Hawfinch** *(below)* is adapted to cracking fruit pits, beech nuts and hornbeam seeds. Its large head and thick neck provide the leverage and muscle to manage its tough food. Conspicuous in flight or on the ground, the Hawfinch has uniquely fanned-out wing feathers and white patches on black wings.

The strikingly plumaged male **Bullfinch** *(right)* is a beautiful bird with a sweet song. Found in hedgerows and orchards of the European countryside, the Bullfinch has a slighter beak than the Hawfinch and is adapted to cracking seeds with thinner coats. It also eats buds, berries and insects.

The **Greenfinch** *(opposite, top)* has a pointed bill, designed for eating insects and fruit in addition to buds and seeds. During the summer they are found in gardens and farm lands, especially where evergreens are present. Large numbers of Greenfinches flock together after breeding is completed. Their undulating flight is a characteristic sight across northern Europe as they migrate into the southwest. The **Pine Siskin** *(opposite, bottom)* has a slightly slimmer bill than the Greenfinch, which allows it to eat pine and birch seeds. A high musical twitter accompanies the Siskin flocks as they fly buoyantly over the countryside.

SOUTH ASIA

Forty million years ago, the Indian subcontinent collided with the Eurasian continental plate. The merger of two continents formed the Himalaya mountains, which isolated the Indian and South Asian avifauna from the Eurasian avifauna.

Asia is relatively flat south of the Himalaya foothills. The Indian deserts merge into the plains of central India and continue east to the Ganges delta. The seasonal lakes of northern India flood with water during the monsoon rains and support vast numbers of breeding waders and migrant Eurasian water birds. The subtropical hardwood forests of Burma and Thailand intergrade with the lowland tropical rain forests of Malaysia and Indonesia. Birds common to the region include parrots, pigeons, hornbills and leafbirds. Migrants from Eurasia cross over the great mountain ranges and also migrate along the coast. As many as five million shorebirds migrate along the east Asian coast, one of the most endangered migratory flyways because of land reclamation and hunting.

Farther south, the Philippine and Indonesian islands are stepping-stones between the Asian and Australasian regions. Many of the major islands were part of the Asian landmass until rising waters flooded the lowlands after the last ice age. Consequently, the avifauna reflects that of the Asian mainland. However, further east lies the Wallace Line, a biological demarcation where Australasian avifauna replaces the Asian avifauna. It was here that the continental plate of Australasia drifted into the Asian plate. The Wallace Line passes between the islands of Bali and Lombok, islands just 15 miles apart, yet ornithologically speaking, continents apart. Barbets, woodpeckers and Laughing Thrushes exist in Bali but are absent on Lombok. Similarly, Cockatoos, honeyeaters and Brush Turkeys are present on Lombok but absent on Bali.

Southeast Asia, especially the islands stretching to Australia, is blanketed in humid tropical rain forests. The rain forest is the oldest and most stable environment on Earth, having remained unaffected by cold during the ice ages. Because organisms have been evolving for many millenia unaffected by adverse climates, the greatest diversity of plant and animal species exists in tropical forests. Most of the bird species live in the treetops, hundreds of feet above the forest floor. Few birds are seen, only their calls are heard. The songs of babblers, trillers and laughing thrushes punctuate the forest darkness.

South Asia is the home of the pheasant tribe, a family of birds with metallic and iridescent plumage, including the ancestor of man's most valuable bird, the **Chicken**, otherwise known as the Red Junglefowl.

Aside from the domestic chicken, perhaps the best known Asian bird is the **Ring-necked Pheasant** *(left)*, introduced around the world

At right: A Java Sparrow *(top)* and a Sarus Crane *(bottom)*.

from its original range in China. The Pheasant is polygamous, that is, each male has a harem of several females. The female sits tight on the eggs, but has the unnerving habit of exploding into flight underfoot. This defensive behavior is effective, but nevertheless, this popular game bird has suffered depredations because of overhunting throughout its ranges.

Humes' Pheasant *(right)* lives on grassy slopes near forests in China, India and Thailand. This beautiful bird has been hunted for food and its feathers; thus it is rarely found near human habitation. The beautiful **Mikado Pheasant** *(opposite, top)*, a native of the island of Taiwan, is also very rare in the wild. The Pheasant Trust of England has been releasing captive birds in areas where they are rare. **White-eared Pheasants** *(below)* have tufts of feathers growing around their eyes. These large pheasants are brown plumaged.

During his courtship display, the male **Golden Pheasant** *(opposite, bottom)* pulls a cape of feathers across his face, then raises his golden hackles. He drops one wing and jumps from side to side while courting the drab female. Males engage in territorial combat, which consists of leap-frogging each other. Originally from central China, the Golden Pheasant, like the Ring-necked Pheasant, has been introduced to Britain and is a common bird in captivity.

Lady Amherst's Pheasant *(opposite, top left)* lives in the rocky foothills of the Himalayas and in Burma, particularly favoring bamboo thickets and fern-covered hillsides. Winter snows may force this bird to move to lower elevations, where it forms small flocks. The crimson-colored **Temmich's Tragopan** *(below)* is a short-tailed pheasant confined to the higher elevations of the Himalayas. Its iridescent plumage is resplendent. The rusty-hued **Blyth's Tragopan** is another of the four stocky species of Asia.

The peacock, the male **Common Peafowl** *(opposite, top right and bottom)*, greets the dawn with loud, raucous cries, and dances for the peahen by shaking his magnificent six-foot feathered train. The Peafowl is considered sacred by Hindus and is the national bird of India. It is common in zoos and gardens but its native habitat is the subtropical hardwood forests of India. The peacock is ever alert for prowling tigers. If a tiger does pounce on its tail, the feathers pull out as the peacock flies to safety.

The plump **Black Francolin** *(right)* is a game bird prized where found in arid India and the Near East. The Francolin prefers grasslands near rivers and wooded areas. Each evening the male calls from his perch and is answered by males calling from their territory. The drab female tends the grass nest and produces six to eight eggs. This species has been introduced as a gamebird to other tropical countries such as Hawaii and Guam.

The **Crested Green Wood Partridge** *(right)* is a crimson crested, rotund bird found in the bamboo and dense tropical rain forests of Indonesia. It keeps hidden by blending in with the shadows. Pairs build a domed nest and lay eight to ten eggs. Both parents scratch leaf litter for fruit, seeds and insects to feed the chicks.

Numerous pigeons and doves populate south Asia. One of the most numerous is the **Peaceful Dove** *(opposite, top)*, a small terrestrial bird of urban as well as rural areas. Like most doves, it builds a flimsy stick nest and lays several cream-colored eggs. The young are fed regurgitated 'pigeon milk' by the female. The **Spotted Dove** appears to be a slightly larger version, big enough to be hunted for food. The spotted dove wears a 'necklace' of dots. It feeds on the ground, eating grains, as well as some insects.

One of the strangest doves is the **Nicobar Pigeon** *(below)*. This species occurs on islands off Southeast Asia and inhabits the shadowy understory of rain forests, where it forages on fallen fruits and insects found under leaves. It is characterized by a very short, white tail, a metallic sheen to the plumage, a hair-like collar of feathers and a nobbed bill.

In the wetlands of Asia, many water birds find refuge from the Arctic winter. Birds that nest in the myriad tundra pools and ponds of Eurasia migrate across the mountains and along the coast. **Bar-headed Geese** *(opposite, bottom)* nest in north central Asia and winter throughout marshlands in Burma and India. Mountain climbers have observed geese migrating above 35,000 feet in the frigid, rarefied air of the Himalayas. How they can fly in the thin, oxygen-poor air without freezing their eyes remains a mystery.

Ruddy Sheldrake *(opposite, bottom left)* and **Red-crested Pochard** are species that commonly nest in Eurasia. These colorful ducks spend the winters in flocks along tropical rivers and marshes of southern Asia.

The little-known **Philippine Duck** *(right)* is found only in the Philippine Islands where it is widespread, but not common, in lowland marshes, ponds and rivers. The species evidently descended from the Mallard-like Chinese Spot-billed Duck. Both sexes are similarly colored.

The **Mandarin Duck** *(below)* of eastern Asia and Japan belongs to the perching duck tribe, the Cairininae. Perching ducks have long, sharp, strong claws and a well-developed hind toe which is not lobed. Noted for their striking plumage and peculiar whistling note in their call, they make their nests in hollow trees. The species is unfortunately threatened with the loss of their nesting habitat by forest logging, removal of hollow trees near secluded ponds and destruction of wooded streams. However, they are frequently kept and raised in captivity. In Japanese culture, the Mandarin Duck is a symbol of marriage fidelity. Hybridizing is common among closely related duck species, but the Mandarin Duck has an aberrant genetic complement, making hybridizing impossible, even in captivity: they may swap mates but have never bred with other species.

In the Indian culture, the **Sarus Crane** *(opposite top and bottom right)* is a symbol of marriage fidelity. The courtship dance of these

five-foot tall cranes is accompanied with much bowing, jumping and trumpeting. This behavior bonds pairs for life. Two or three eggs are laid on a nest of vegetation in wetlands across India and south Asia. Cranes migrate from their breeding grounds in the Chinese marshes to India over the Himalaya Mountains.

Java Sparrows *(opposite)* use their stout beaks to crack fruit pits and seeds. Common in Java and Bali, they have been introduced as cage birds into neighboring Malaysia and other tropical countries, where some have escaped and become agricultural pests in cultivated rice fields. The Java Sparrow's courtship display consists of the male bending over and bouncing up and down while sidling ever nearer to his intended mate. They lay three to eight eggs in a domed-shaped nest in trees and buildings eaves.

Golden-fronted Leafbirds *(below)* have shining orange foreheads and blue throats. Because of their beauty, they are sometimes kept as cage birds. Flocks of leafbirds forage in the thick foliage of deciduous tropical trees for small insects. While their calls are simple, golden-fronted leafbirds can be superb mimics.

Giant Pittas *(right)* are stocky, long-legged birds with bright plumage on their undersides and somber plumage on top. The birds hide by simply turning their backs to the observer. Pittas have a keen sense of smell and have strong bills for eating snails and worms. They take captured snails to a favorite rock and, using it like an anvil, crack the snail shells on it. Giant Pittas reside in lowland tropical forests and build a domed nest of moss and rootlets where they lay three to five eggs.

White-crested Laughing Thrushes *(right)* are large, robust, jay-like birds that emit raucous cries. Individuals in the flock pick up and repeat the call until the surrounding forest resounds with laughter. One ornithologist describes the sound of laughing thrushes as like 'a chorus of diabolical cackling laughter and an orchestra of mournful, weepy piping.'

Black-naped Orioles *(opposite, top right)* are common in second-growth woods and forests throughout Asia, India and the islands stretching to Australia. These robust birds are fruit and insect eaters and have a melodious loud song.

Hill Mynas *(below)* are familiar to most people as the talking birds of pet stores. While not capable of building sentences, they mimic passersby, whistle rudely, and are quite smart and alert to any changes in their environment. They range across India into Southeast Asia. Occasional escaped pets have taken up residence in Hong Kong parks.

The white-crested **Rothschild Myna** *(opposite, top left)* is an endangered species in its native habitat on Bali, but exists in zoo collections in significant numbers. It nests in tree cavities and under roofs.

Black Drongos *(opposite, bottom)* are noisy and aggressive and will not hesisate to attack large animals, including men, in defense of their saucer-shaped nests. Drongo species are distinguished by their elongated tail feathers, which they use for stability in flight. They are acrobatic fliers as they 'hawk' insects from their perches or drive them to the ground.

House Crows *(opposite)* are opportunistic omnivores. They will eat almost anything, including cattle ticks and human garbage. Their catholic tastes enable the crows to become so successful that they are a pest species in some areas. House Crows have been introduced to other parts of the world, including Africa and Australia, where they wreak havoc by killing other native wildlife and spreading disease. Major control efforts are required to reduce their populations.

The **Monkey-Eating Eagle** *(right)* of the Philippines is the largest eagle species. Its highly arched beak and feathered mane add to its ferocious appearance. The monkey-eating eagle is found only in the extensive, undisturbed rain forests of the Philippine Islands, where they are critically endangered. Perhaps as few as 50 pairs remain. Rain forests are being harvested at an alarming rate and the remaining eagles are sought by collectors. This eagle needs protected areas of extensive rain forest where they can pluck monkeys off branches and take hornbills for food.

Rhinoceros Hornbills *(below)* are very large birds that are found in the primary tropical rainforests. Hornbills nest in tree holes. The male walls the female into the nest cavity with guano and a substance secreted by his stomach. The nestlings and female are fed by the male through a crack in the wall until they are large enough to evade predators. Considered good luck to the native people of

Borneo, hornbills are often kept as pets and will follow their masters around like dogs.

The **Northern Pied Hornbill** *(opposite)* of India and Malaysia glides through the forest canopy with its great wings making a whooshing sound. Its enormous but lightweight bill is perforated with numerous canals. The hornbill is primarily a fruit eater, but will also eat frogs and snakes.

Looking like a long-billed woodpecker crossed with a ground jay, the **Hoopoo** *(right)* is unmistakable. Named for its hooping call, this bird was considered magic by the ancients. Brewed potions of hoopoo parts were prescribed to aid eyesight and stimulate memory. This peculiar bird is found in dry scrublands across Asia, Africa and Europe. The Hoopoo eats ants, termites and lizards caught on the ground. Unlike its fastidious hornbill relatives, the Hoopoo keeps a messy nest in tree hollows.

Short-tailed Albatrosses *(below)* are perhaps the rarest of sea birds. Once common across the North Pacific, their numbers were reduced to near extinction by Japanese feather hunters and volcanic eruptions on their nesting islands off southern Japan. The Short-tailed Albatross population has slowly returned to about 250 birds, and they are reinhabiting previous island habitats. Albatrosses take seven years

to mature and lay only one egg annually, but can live as long as 70 years.

Bonin Petrels *(below)* form strong pair bonds that are maintained by billing and cooing after dark on the breeding grounds where they nest in burrows. They are named for the Bonin Islands of Japan where these sea birds nest. Petrels are related to albatrosses and share the characteristic tubenoses of the family. Tubes atop the bill shed excess salt, permitting the birds to drink seawater without dehydrating.

Sooty Storm-petrels *(opposite)* inhabit the crevices of rocky cliffs and boulder fields on the Bonin Islands. These sea birds are diminutive versions of albatrosses and are equally vulnerable to disturbance. Because they are so small, they spend the day at sea and return to land after dark to avoid predators. They feed by holding their wings out to catch the wind and, pattering with their webbed feet, pick marine insects and tiny squid from the surface.

Crested Terns *(right)* breed on the islets and sandbars that are scattered throughout Southeast Asia and the tropical Pacific. These sea birds rely on islands undisturbed by man for breeding. Crested tern populations are greatly depleted by humans, who steal their eggs. Terns feed on small fish seized while plunging from great heights. During early courtship, the male tern captures a fish and presents it to the female.

AUSTRALASIA

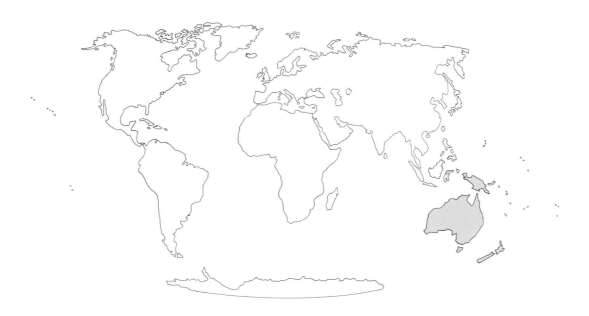

Australia and the mountainous islands of New Guinea and New Zealand compose the bioregion known as Australasia. Once part of the supercontinent Gondwandland that included Antarctica, Africa and South America, Australia broke off and drifted east quite early in bird evolution. Thus, it retains some bird families considered more primitive than other families that evolved later. New Zealand then fragmented and drifted from Australia. So New Zealand retains even more primitive species — such as the extinct moas — than Australia. Standing 10 feet tall, they were flightless giants that existed until early Polynesian colonists exterminated them. A small version still exists today; the kiwi of New Zealand.

Australia is a relatively flat, dry continent. The interior, known as the 'outback,' is desert, dry woodlands and grasslands. But it was once lush tropical forests. As the climate grew more arid, bird populations were isolated in the remnant rain forests. Today, the forests fringing the coasts in northeast Australia provide the only habitat for tropical species like the birds of paradise and cassowaries. Altogether, Australia hosts about 745 bird species that breed or visit.

While much smaller, New Guinea has 725 species of birds. It is a mountainous, tropical country that was once completely forested. Bird species had opportunities to evolve because populations were isolated by mountains. Birds of paradise evolved many fantastic species, and only a few of the less colorful species reached Australia. New Zealand is also mountainous, but lies in a temperate zone. It has only 305 species.

Islands between Australia and Asia have been used as 'stepping-stones' for flying birds to colonize the Australian continent. Some species range into Indonesia to the Wallace Line between Bali and Lombok. This is the boundary that separates the south Asian from the Australasian avifauna.

The only bird capable of killing a man is the **Double-wattled Cassowary** *(left and right bottom)*! Weighing up to 130 lb, it carries a stiletto-like claw on its foot and can disembowel a human with its powerful kick. Cassowaries are kept as pets in New Guinea and are involved in many incidents of this nature. The New Guineans value cassowaries for trading; one bird may fetch more than $1000! The feathers are used for art and the bones for daggers.

The smaller **Bennet's Cassowary** is found in the mountains of New Guinea and uses its helmet to part vegetation as it runs headlong into the rain forest. The male tends the clutch of green eggs deposited in a ground nest by the female. The cassowaries will commonly take to water and swim with it sticking above the surface.

The related **Emu** *(right top)* is found on the open plains of the outback, where it runs at speeds reaching 35 mph. These large, flightless birds are distant relatives of the African ostrich and suggest that these continents were once connected. How else could large, flightless birds get to Australia?

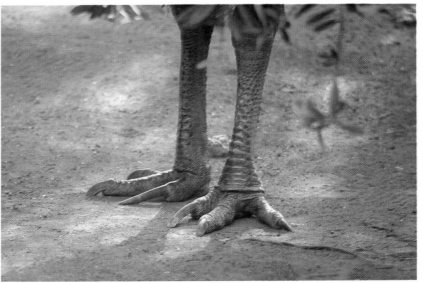

The **Brown Kiwi** *(right)* of New Zealand is a unique flightless, and nocturnal, bird. Fur-like feathers cloak its rotund body. It has a long, probing bill with nostrils at the tip for smelling out worms and stout legs for scratching away leaf litter. The kiwi lays the largest egg of any bird in relation to its body size. With protection, the kiwi is becoming more common in patches of uncut native bush. With great affection, the people of New Zealand have chosen the kiwi as their national bird and often refer to themselves as kiwis.

Penguins are completely flightless, aquatic birds of southern polar oceans and adjacent seas. With dense plumage, torpedo-shaped bodies and wings modified into flippers for swimming, they are well adapted to life in the cold waters. Three species live in Australia and New Zealand.

Yellow-eyed Penguins *(opposite)* are the rarest penguin, for their world-wide population numbers only several thousand. Yet they are readily seen on the southern islands of New Zealand, where they come ashore to nest in shoreline vegetation. Here, they come into contact with farmers' dogs and cats, a threat to their diminishing population.

Little Blue Penguins *(below)* are the smallest penguin species

and also the most readily seen. Large numbers come ashore to nest on the coasts of southern Australia and New Zealand. Little Blue Penguins can be heard, if not seen, at night, braying in their nests under boathouses or docks. Two eggs are laid and guarded for several months. To feed the growing youngsters, parents swim out to sea daily to gather shrimp.

Fiordland Crested Penguins (*right*) belong to a group whose distribution reaches New Zealand from the islands of Antarctica. This species nests on the rugged coasts of southern New Zealand in cavities under heavy coastal shrubs. The parents feed on crustacea at sea and return to land to feed their two chicks.

The remarkable migration of the **Short-tailed Shearwaters** (*below*) describes a clockwise movement across virtually the entire Pacific Ocean. Shearwaters nest in burrows dug into islets off the coast of Australia and Tasmania. After nesting, they travel north, following the east coast of Asia, and reach the offshore waters of Alaska in the summer. Upwelling nutrients nourish swarms of crustacea, and tens of millions of shearwaters concentrate to feed on the abundant food. Winter drives the birds down the west coast of North America. South of California, the shearwaters angle southwest and return to their breeding grounds, completing a voyage of more than 20,000 miles in one year.

Black Petrels (*opposite*) are related to shearwaters, but are stockier and certainly much rarer. The endangered Black Petrel breeds on a few small islands in New Zealand, where its population

is threatened by the cats and weasels that have been introduced to the area in modern times. Black Petrels exhibit a migration pattern similar to that of that of the shearwater, but instead of entering the North Pacific, they winter off Panama, where it is thought they once passed into the Gulf of Mexico, when sea levels were higher. This ancient migration instinct is still present and useful for these sea birds.

Darters *(opposite, top)*, like their cormorant relatives, are aquatic species. In slow-moving streams, Darters submerge themselves to spear prey underwater. Once fish are stabbed with their pointed bills, Darters will surface and swallow the fish headfirst to avoid the spines. Darters lack waterproofing oil glands and must hang their wings in the sun to dry.

Australian Gannets *(right and opposite bottom)* are torpedo-shaped sea birds that feed by plunging into the ocean. When a school of fish is sighted, gannets half close their wings and plummet toward their targeted prey. Onshore, gannets nest in colonies, where they usually lay one egg per pair. Immature birds attain the snow-white adult plumage in three to four years and may breed after six years.

Brown Boobies *(below)* are a tropical species that tends to dive in shallower water than gannets or other booby species. Called boobies because of their genetic tameness, they build a stick nest on the ground on islands throughout Australasia. They are most common on islands without predators or human disturbances.

Silver Gulls *(below and opposite top)* are common in Australia and New Zealand, where they frequent harbors and bays to scavenge fish offal and garbage. Known by their red legs and bills, these dainty gulls nest on isolated headlands and islands.

Straw-necked Ibises *(opposite, bottom right)* forage in inland marshes and fields of Australia and nest in colonies in rushes and rank vegetation. By hunting foods such as toads and grasshoppers, they have earned the moniker 'farmer's friend.' Ibises are sedentary, but in times of drought they will become nomadic, flying in 'Vs' to find new water sources and associated prey.

Watching motionlessly, **White-faced Herons** *(opposite, bottom left)* hunt for aquatic prey in freshwater habitats in Australia. When flying, they pull their necks into a hunched position. Occasionally they have wandered to New Guinea and southeast Asia, and individuals colonized New Zealand in the 1940s.

Black Swans *(right)* are native to Australia but have been introduced to New Zealand and Europe. However, these swans never became established in Europe because they were believed to be birds of the devil. The Black Swan, and its close relative, the Mute Swan, are stunning-looking birds, and are quite popular as attractions in waterfowl collections. In interior Australia, Black Swans follow the rains and nest in temporary lakes. In drought conditions, the birds migrate great distances to find water.

Cape Barren Geese (*right*) breed on islands off southern Australia. The geese migrate to the mainland to feed on grasses and forage among the sheep. Local sheep ranchers persecuted the birds in the belief that sheep would not feed near them. Under protection, the birds are becoming numerous again. The Cape Barren Goose is an aberrant goose, perhaps a primitive relative of the shelduck. It prefers to remain dry and avoids water.

Burdekin Shelducks (*below*) are found in brackish coastal waters in tropical Australia. They feed along the water's edge, moving upriver in dry periods. Tree holes lined with down are used for nesting. Six to 12 creamy-white eggs are laid in the nest. After hatching, the young must jump from the nest hole to the water below.

The **Lotusbird** or **Lily-trotter** (*opposite, top and bottom*) has exceptionally long toes that enable it to walk over marsh vegetation without sinking. It hunts snails and insect larvae on the undersides of water lillies. This species has reversed sex roles. The male builds the nest on a floating pile of marsh vegetation and defends it with a trumpet-like alarm cry. The female lays four eggs with brown splotches and interlacing lines, and the male completes the incubation duties. The long-toed young can walk on lily pads a day after hatching.

Australian Spur-winged Plovers inhabit grasslands near airport runways, croplands and marshes. These shy birds are

difficult to approach without attracting their attention. When alerted, they repeatedly give an alarm call, alerting other birds in the vicinity. Yellow wattles grow from the bases of their bills and mask their faces. The birds retain a primitive characteristic spur on the wrist of each wing.

Found solely in New Guinea, the **Victoria Crowned Pigeon** *(right)*, is the largest member of the pigeon family and one of the most ornate. Its laterally compressed head plumes are used in a 'nodding' display during courtship. This huge bird forages on the rain forest floor for fruit and insects. When disturbed, it ponderously flaps its wings, attempting to get into the trees overhead. Once there, it flicks its tail up and down to maintain balance.

Imperial Pigeons *(below)* are large, tree-dwelling species that seldom come to the ground. They forage on fruit pulp and nuts. **Orange-bellied Fruit Doves** are also arboreal, and in spite of their colorful plumage, are difficult to observe in the dense tree foliage. These gregarious pigeons feed frequently near towns in mangroves and fig trees.

Australasia abounds with parrots of all sizes and colors. One of the most abundant is the **Galah** *(opposite)*, a large gray and pink cockatoo favored as a pet by many Australians. This well-known bird of open woodlands and adjacent plains is somewhat nomadic. After breeding, pairs join large flocks of hundreds of birds. A flock overhead lets its presence be known by much loud shrieking. The Galah forages in forests and farm lands, eating seeds, fruits, berries, nuts and tubers.

Major Mitchell's Cockatoo has a crest that it raises when excited to reveal hidden colors. Its heavy, curved beak is used for cracking seeds and manipulating fruit rinds, and the coordination between its feet, beak and tongue is remarkable.

The largest cockatoo species is the slate-black **Palm Cockatoo** *(opposite, bottom right)*, found in the rain forests of New Guinea and northeast Australia. They nest in tree holes and lay two to five round eggs. Unfortunately, this magnificent species is very rare because of unscrupulous collecting for the pet store trade.

Red Electus Parrots *(below)* confounded scientists for many years because the difference in color is so extreme between the sexes. The green males were thought to be a different species than the red females. They are found in the rain forests of New Guinea.

Turquoise Parrots *(opposite, top)* are limited to sections of the dry forests of Australia, where they are increasingly rare. Though not yet endangered, increased logging in their habitats could threaten their populations with extinction. **Ornate Lorikeets** *(opposite, bottom left)* have brushlike tongues designed for removing pollen and nectar from flowers.

Crimson Rosellas *(right)* are brilliantly colored parrots found in forests near towns in northeastern Australia. They feed on or near the ground, searching for seeds, fruits and nuts. Pairs seek tree holes in which to breed, making a nest of powdered wood and laying several round, white eggs. The name 'rosella' derives from what the early

Australian colonists called these birds—'rose hillers.' The name was shortened and thus evolved into a unique Australian name for a unique Australian bird.

Keas (*below and opposite bottom*) are bold parrots of the New Zealand mountains and the only parrots to forage in the snow. Keas nest under rocky ledges and in burrows protected from the cold and rain. These birds tend their chicks carefully, grooming them with their beaks. In their homeland, debate continues over their reputation as sheep killers, although wildlife experts maintain that such a belief is unfounded. But for more than a century, at least 150,000 were killed by bounty hunters. Today, Keas are protected and have become fearless and very curious about human objects, even going so far as to sample the rubber wiper blades of cars and to rob campers.

One of the rarest birds in the world is the **Kakapo** (*right*) of New Zealand. Also called the 'owl-parrot' because of its unique habits, the Kakapo is flightless, lives in an underground burrow and comes out only at night to waddle among the grasses and herbs that form its diet. Only 50 remain in New Zealand because imported predators, such as weasels and cats killed many of the ground-nesting Kakapo. Recently, a major effort has been made to provide the remaining Kakapos with a safe haven on Little Barrier Island.

Tawny Frogmouths (*opposite, top photos*) have large gaping mouths surrounded by bristles. At night they sit on low branches and drop on small animals passing below. During daylight, frogmouths are found in woodlands with large, spreading trees, where they perch upright and resemble dead tree snags.

Yellow-breasted Sunbirds *(below)* are the jewels of the garden. The birds flit flower to flower using their scimitar-shaped bills to gather nectar and insects. Pendulous nests are woven at the extremities of branches and tended by the females.

The **Laughing Kookaburra** *(right)* is the largest kingfisher of Australasia. Unlike most kingfishers, it lives away from water in the dry woodlands and is a common sight in the rural towns of Australia. Sitting atop a telephone pole, the kookaburra will suddenly drop on a lizard, snake or large insect, bashing it to death with its heavy bill. The laugh of the kookaburra should be familiar to anyone who has ever watched a jungle movie. Its weird call is often the only 'jungle noise' on the soundtrack!

The **Papuan Hornbill** *(opposite)* is a resident in the rain forest treetops from New Guinea to Burma. Traveling far above the ground, the hornbill's raucous call can be heard a great distance. The Papuan Hornbill nests in tree cavities. The female is sealed into the cavity with mud and dung collected by the male. For the duration of incubation, he feeds her fruits, insects and reptiles through a crack. This isolation is designed to protect her from marauding predators such as snakes and monkeys. When captured as a chick, a hornbill becomes quite tame and makes an excellent pet. However, it rarely mates in captivity and cannot add to a population that continues to diminish as rain forests are destroyed.

Rarely seen, more often heard, **Bare-faced Crows** *(right)* are the voices of the rain forest. Its high-pitched, nasal caw reverberates through the forest. Like most crows, they travel in flocks among the trees and at the forest's edge, coming down to the riverside to scavenge fallen fruit and animal matter.

Named for a loud cry, **Whistling Kites** *(opposite, bottom)* are usually found near water, where they hunt insects, fish, amphibians and dead animals. Whistling Kites soar lazily on long, bowed wings and forked tails. Often roosting in pairs or groups, Whistling Kites — or eagles, as they are also called — blend easily into the lush foliage of the forest.

Flocks of several hundred **White-breasted Wood Swallows** festoon tree branches and wires near the coast. They reside in open areas near the coasts of Australasia, where they flock together and make passing forays against marauding hawks and crows.

Australian Thrushes *(opposite, top right)* feed on the ground and in low branches in forests and wood lots. These solitary birds seldom move far from their territories, which they proclaim by singing. They nest in large trees and build bowl-shaped nests.

Gould Finches *(below)* are paintbox-colored cage birds popular around the world but native to the dry grassland savannas of northern Australia. Like many bird species in the dry outback, Gould Finches migrate during the rainy season in search of new nesting grounds.

Splendid Fairy Wrens *(opposite, top left)* frequent dense undergrowths and gardens in Australia. Their cocked tails and blue colors add a bold measure of distinction to these diminutive birds. Family helpers are common. As many as five adults have been observed visiting the same domed nest to care for the chicks.

Red and black with white wingbars and forehead, the **Scarlet Robin** *(opposite)* is a conspicuous resident of the open forests of southern Australia in the breeding season. It moves to dense forests, forming small groups during the winter. It is found on islands in the southwest Pacific, including Tasmania.

With long, curved bills, **White-cheeked Honeyeaters** *(right)* probe blossoms for nectar and insects. The honeyeater family is widespread and successful in Australia, with 70 species represented. They also have colonized islands as far away as Hawaii. They build domed nests and feed the chicks insects with a drop of nectar.

Birds of paradise and the related bowerbirds are known for their elaborate breeding strategies. Birds of paradise rely on their fantastic plumages and breeding displays to attract mates, while the less colorful bowerbirds craft display grounds. Inhabiting treetops in high mountain ranges, the **Princess Stephania Bird of Paradise** *(below)* carries two-foot long tail feathers much sought after by New Guinea tribesmen.

These birds, along with the **Red-plumaged Bird of Paradise**, have been hunted to a point where populations have been eliminated from some areas of New Guinea. Feather plumes and wings adorn many native headdresses, making them some of the most beautiful in the world. These birds use their colorful plumage to compete for mates. Males assemble at specific trees for a group mating dance. At this time, the back feathers and wings are exposed in full display, revealing the true splendor of the birds' plumage. Females also appear and choose the best dancer for mating.

Lacking feathers as gorgeous as those of the birds of paradise, bowerbirds rely on elaborate constructions to attract mates. Generally, the more drab the bowerbird species, the more ornate the bower, and those bowerbirds with the greatest color difference between the sexes tend to build the most elaborate bowers. For example, the **Satin Bowerbird** *(right and below)* builds a bower which is decorated with blue objects all the same hue. Anything that is the correct hue, including plastic razors and pens, will be gathered for display. The male then picks up a blue object and waves it before the female to entice her into the bower for mating. The blue-eyed female tends the nest and nestlings alone.

Bedecked in gold and black, the male **Regent Bowerbird** *(opposite, top)* is one of the most attractive bowerbird species. In the moist rain forests of northern Australia, the male builds a display avenue by placing many sticks upright on both sides of a path. He then plasters the walls with a mixture of saliva and fruit pulp and decorates the ground with colorful berries and flowers to attract the female into the bower, where mating occurs.

Brush Turkeys *(opposite, bottom)* are unique among Australasian birds. Their breeding behaviors are reptile-like but show ingenuity at the same time. The birds rely on natural sources of heat to incubate their eggs. Brush Turkeys scrape together a large pile of dirt and dead leaves. Through bacterial action, the decaying vegetation gives off enough heat to incubate the eggs. To ensure that the eggs do not cook, the male brush turkey periodically senses the degree of warmth with his naked head. If it is too hot, he removes the cover. If it is too cool, he adds more. The young dig their own way out.

OCEANIA

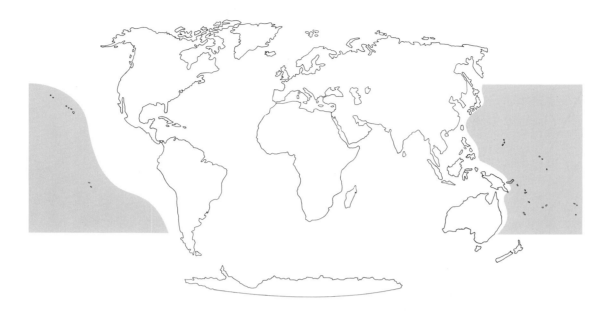

T he vast reaches of the Pacific Ocean are dotted with islands which are oases of life for terrestrial creatures. Once a species arrives, either because of a storm or purposeful travel, it may evolve over time into several other species to take full advantage of the lack of competition. The distances between the continents and islands are a barrier to most bird movement; thus many of the Pacific islands have few species of birds, but a high proportion of unique species.

For example, the islands of Hawaii are the most isolated land in the world, more than 3000 miles from any continent or other major island group. From one ancestor reaching Hawaii, there arose more than 40 new species and subspecies. The birds here are truly the result of a natural experiment in evolution continuing to this day. Unfortunately, many are endangered or extinct. Island birds have usually evolved without predators because mammals and reptiles cannot survive the great ocean distances to colonize new islands. So when normative predators are introduced by man, their predation profoundly depletes naive, native bird species.

The high islands of the Pacific are formed by volcanoes. They are generally wet and well forested, and are populated with birds that have immigrated from the Asian and Australian continents. Hawaii has received birds from North America also. The flat islands are remnants of high islands eroded to sea level. They are typically very dry with little vegetation.

On the uninhabited atolls and islands scattered across the Pacific, the seafowl rookeries are the most obvious signs of the wealth of marine life. Sea birds require only a piece of land above the winter storms, provided they are predator free. This will be a habitat for myriad nesting sea birds, with some nesting in trees, some in cliffs, and others on the ground or under the ground.

A sea bird colony is a riot of confusion with every space utilized. Likewise, the ocean's resources are partitioned. Different species have evolved to hunt in different areas of the sea. Some birds are surface feeders, others are plunge divers, inshore dippers or open ocean skimmers; all the areas are used for fishing.

Laysan Albatross *(left and right bottom)* are common only in the northwestern Hawaiian Islands. These are the 'goony birds' of Midway Island, although that is a poor name for these tame, beautiful and intelligent birds who can return to their exact nest sites and mate year after year for 25 years or more!

Albatrosses feed nocturnally on squid and flying fish eggs. **Black-footed Albatrosses** *(right top)* spend much of their lives at sea, flying on gale force winds, cruising behind vessels, or roaming the Bering Sea. When they return to land after a long period, they have difficulty adjusting to a hard landing surface and often crash. A single egg is laid and tended by both parents, and the chick takes six months before it leaves the roost.

Wedge-tailed Shearwaters *(right)* are smaller versions of albatrosses. They locate food by smelling faint odors with their unique tube noses. After their nightly feeding, they return to their tropical island breeding grounds. Eerie cries that sound like babies wailing or cats fighting emanate from their underground burrows.

The **Great Frigatebird** *(opposite)* is renowned for its courtship display. The male inflates his red balloon throat and rattles and drums his beak on the pouch to attract the attention of females. The frigatebird has earned the name 'Man O' War bird' because it tips up the tails of terns and boobies in flight, making them drop their captured fish. The Frigatebird has the greatest wing surface to body weight ratio of all birds. The aerodynamic design of its wings enables the frigatebird to soar for hours, even days. However, it cannot settle on the ocean, for it lacks webbed feet and the capacity to get airborne if it becomes wet.

Sooty Terns *(below)* are like small Frigatebirds; they cannot land on water, but are so expert at flying that they sleep on the wing! They lead an aerial existence, dipping down to the sea to take squid and fish, but staying airborne for six months without touching land until the breeding season. Hundreds of thousands of Sooty Terns arrive at

the colony simultaneously and begin the noisy process of breeding, their vociferous calls earning them the name 'wide-awake' terns.

White Terns (*opposite, top right*) are dainty, fairy-like creatures that have a unique nesting strategy. They dispense with a nest and instead lay a single egg in the crook of a branch. This is to prevent parasites from infesting the chick. Once the egg hatches, the chick clings to its perch with its oversized sharp claws. Looking like a dark version of the white tern, the **Brown Noddy** (*opposite, top left*) nests on the ground. The Noddy is named for its breeding display, in which both partners, with gaping yellow mouths, nod their heads and point to the nest.

Red-tailed Tropicbirds (*right and below*) have their feet placed so far back on their bodies that they can hardly walk on land, but in the air, they are one of the few birds that can fly backward! During aerial breeding displays—usually at the hottest part of the tropical day—they whirl around each other and 'back pedal' to fly in reverse.

The ancestors of the **Nene** (*opposite, bottom*) evidently evolved from Canada goose stock that somehow ended up in Hawaii. But the Nene has shown special adaptations to the rough volcanic slopes where it lives and has partially lost the webbing between its toes common to other water birds. The Nene was once at the brink of extinction after the introduction of mongooses. Luckily, some birds removed to England for breeding were reintroduced into Hawaii to augment the dying population. Today, the birds are surviving with the additional help of captive-reared individuals.

The **Laysan Duck** *(opposite, bottom)* evolved from Mallard ancestors lost on Laysan Island many thousands of years ago. Like the Nene goose, the Laysan Duck has developed unique features of its own. It has lost one flight feather from each wing, demonstrating a tendency toward flightlessness, a condition common to island species without predators. The Laysan Duck lives on a hypersaline lake in the middle of Laysan Island, where it feed on brine flies. Its manner of feeding is to charge through swarms of flies, with its mouth open, swallowing flies on the run.

Guam Kingfishers *(below)* are extinct in the wild because the brown tree snake, introduced from somewhere in Australasia, ate virtually every one of them. A few individuals were captured before they all disappeared down the snakes' gullets. Fortunately, efforts to breed these birds in zoos have been successful, and a small number survive in captivity. However, getting rid of the snakes on Guam has proved more difficult. Until the tree snakes are controlled, the Kingfisher will be a species without a country.

Guam Rails *(right)* are more fortunate than the Guam Kingfishers. Though they suffered the same fate from snakes, the Rails have fared better in zoos and recently have been introduced to a snakeless island north of Guam, where it is hoped they will regain their former numbers.

Mangrove Flycatchers *(opposite, top)* have a broad, flat bill surrounded by bristles that aid in funneling flying insects into their

mouths. These flycatchers perch on a branch in the understory of the forest and sally forth to pluck bugs from the air. These birds are found in forests or mangrove swamps on islands surrounding the South China Sea.

Rufous Fantails *(opposite, bottom)* have colonized the southwest islands of Oceania from Australasia. As they flit from branch to branch chasing insects in the understory of the forest, they cock and spread their long tails. They weave a nest of fibers and grass around a branch to form their nest, in which they lay four eggs.

The **Nihoa Millerbird** *(right)* is a small, nondescript flycatcher that arrived in Hawaii from the Far East. It lives only on Nihoa Island, where its population numbers about 300 birds. As its name suggests, it eats miller moths, which abound on Nihoa. A similar species became extinct on Laysan Island around the turn of the century.

The **Laysan Finch** *(below)* may be the closest relative to the original founding species in Hawaii, believed to be a North American finch. The Laysan Finch survives only on Laysan, but a related species lives on Nihoa Island. This thick-billed finch is adaptable and opportunistic, eating sea bird eggs, grass seeds and carrion.

The crimson **Apapane** *(opposite, top)* is the most common honeyeater in the Hawaiian Islands, and arose from the same ancestor as the Laysan Finch. Always on the move, it probes the blossoms of native trees for nectar. The Apapane is found on all the Hawaiian Islands, usually above two thousand feet above sea level.

ANTARCTICA

The coldest, driest, windiest and darkest continent is the most inhospitable continent for birds. Yet 40 species of sea birds are the only vertebrates besides three species of seals to inhabit the islands and the margins of the frozen continent, gaining sustenance from the sea. However, only a few songbirds and one species of duck can survive in the desolate region.

Antarctica was once a lush, tropical land until the continent drifted to its current position at the South Pole. Ice, snow and harsh wind characterize its climate year-round, but the Antarctic peninsula and sub-Antarctica islands are snow-free for a few summer months. Cold water currents, rich in nutrients, support vast schools of krill, a species of shrimp, that in turn feeds concentrations of sea birds. To complete the food chain, sea birds are eaten by leopard seals.

In this sea bird stronghold, the penguin family best characterizes the south polar avifauna. Propelled by their powerful fore flippers, schools of penguins ply the frigid waters, literally flying beneath and porpoising above the water. Clothed in dense, fur-like feathers and thick blubber, penguins are insulated against the frigid cold and protected against the punishing waves, rocks and ice.

Standing over five feet tall, **Emperor Penguins** *(these pages)* are the largest penguin species, and breed in the most extreme weather conditions of any bird. For about 60 days in the darkness of the Antarctic winter, the male cradles one egg on his feet until it hatches. During this time, he stands immobile in winter cold, huddling with other males to reduce the effects of blizzard conditions. He appears very reluctant to relinquish the chick when the female returns from the sea, but having lost 40 percent of his body weight by fasting, he must feed himself. Both parents feed the chick until midsummer, when it leaves on its own.

95

King Penguins *(below and bottom left)* are slightly smaller than the Emperors. While superficially resembling them, the Kings have more orange on their nape. Males and females share incubation duties. They do not build a nest, but hold a single egg between their abdomen and feet. Chick growth is very slow, so breeding must take place every other year.

Adelie Penguins *(opposite)* share the ice shelf with the Emperor Penguins. Immense colonies of this abundant species are highly gregarious, inquisitive and apparently interested in humans. Adelie Penguins nest around Antarctic research stations and stare with button-shaped eyes at the comings and goings of the scientists. Adelies nest on stony plateaus, often very far from the sea if the shelf ice has not broken close to the sea. They lay two eggs, and if food is plentiful, they can rear both chicks. Penguins feed on krill, an abundant form of shrimp.

Gentoo Penguins *(right and bottom right)* breed on the Antarctic peninsula and sub-Antarctic islands. In contrast to the Adelies, Gentoos are shy and retiring. Also, unlike other penguin species, they nest in scattered colonies that move from year to year. Adults, like most penguins, feed on krill — shrimp-like crustacea found in immense numbers in the waters. While feeding, the penguins may themselves become food for Leopard Seals — predators of the south.

These pages: Adelie Penguins

Macaroni Penguins are medium-sized penguins found on the Antarctic peninsula and the sub-Antarctic South Orkney Islands. Named for the eighteenth century English dandy who 'stuck a feather in his cap and called it macaroni,' these penguins have yellow plumes adorning their crowns. Described as being bolder, tougher and less friendly than other penguins, they also smell goatish and rank.

If the penguins rule the seas, then the albatrosses and petrels dominate the air. The incessant winds sweeping unchecked around the Earth at the lower latitudes carry the stiff-winged, giant albatrosses and smaller petrels. The largest flying birds are the **Wandering Albatrosses** (*opposite, top and bottom*). With 11-foot wingspreads, they grace the seas with their mastery of flight. Their huge, saber-like wings are well suited for gliding on the gales common to Antarctic storms. These great albatrosses do indeed wander across the bottom of the world: one was recorded as having flown 3000 miles in 12 days! These large but tame birds nest in small colonies on grassy swales on sub-Antarctic islands, and raise one chick every other year. The chicks then take nine years to mature before commencing to breed.

No bigger than a starling, the **Wilson's Storm-Petrel** is able to survive the same weather and winds as the tremendous albatross. This diminutive sea bird dances on the water, picking small invertebrates from the surface. It is common on the sub-Antarctic islands, and is perhaps one of the most abundant sea birds in the world.

King Cormorants nest on the Antarctic peninsula in small colonies built on stony headlands. Their nests are seaweed and bones cemented to the rock substrate with guano. The chicks are naked upon hatching and are brooded continuously until downy. Cormorants swim underwater, but unlike penguins, they move their rear feet instead of their wings. The parents dive for fish and feed the chicks by regurgitation.

Sheathbills (*below*) are the only land bird on the continent of Antarctica. Two widely separated species live in the Antarctic — one yellow billed and one black billed. These white, pigeon-like birds can fly, but prefer to run around on unwebbed feet. They are scavengers, eating dead birds and eggs, often sticking their heads into the bloody carcasses of seals.

AFRICA

The African continent is the Old World tropics, site of origin for many bird families and home to more than 1500 breeding species. Africa is also the wintering ground for Eurasian migrants escaping the harsh arctic weather. Africa is characterized by hot temperatures and seasonal rains in an otherwise dry climate. The dominant vegetation types are grasslands and isolated trees and scrub. African ground birds are conspicuous components of these habitats and easier to view than on other continents. Ostriches, guinea fowl, cranes, secretary birds and vultures are easily observed in national parks.

The North African coast borders the Mediterranean Sea and is considered to be part of Eurasia. The dry scrub habitat that surrounds the sea slowly intergrades into the vast Sahara-Sahel desert. This area is a major barrier to birds migrating from Europe. To the south and east of the great desert, scrub woodlands and savanna grasslands intergrade into the subtropical and tropical forests of central Africa. The wetter climate results from the prevailing moisture-laden winds moving inland off the Atlantic Ocean. The belt of humid rain forest that girdles equatorial Africa is rich in birds, but the dense vegetation makes bird observation extremely difficult. Touracos, superb starlings and thrushes are characteristic species. Rainfall diminishes across western and southern Africa. Dry woodlands replace tropical forests where they have not already been felled by man. Woodland birds include bushshrikes, weaver finches and bee-eaters.

Snow-capped Mount Kilimanjaro punctuates the equatorial region. On the mist-shrouded slopes grow mountain forests and alpine vegetation. Sunbirds pollinate giant species of asters. The elevated terrain near the Rift Valley is the headwater for several river drainages. The wetlands of the Rift Valley's Lake Tanganyika, Lake Victoria and upper Nile valleys provide freshwater marsh habitats for herons, storks, cranes, ducks, plovers and kingfishers. Other areas of importance include the seasonal wetlands dotting the savanna woodlands and grasslands. Birds migrate within these regions, following the rainy season and crops of insects and seeds that result. Flocks of the Red-billed Quelea, a grain-eating bird, sometimes reach plague proportions.

Offshore lies the large island of Madagascar and the smaller Mascarene, Seychelles and Comoros islands. These islands were once home to a unique assemblage of bird species. Here, the famous dodo and gargantuan 'elephant birds' lived until man colonized the islands, bringing predacious rats, cats and pigs. Some of the rarest birds in the world hang onto a precarious existence on these islands.

Islands off the south coast of Africa are bathed by cold water currents from the Antarctic. Colonies of penguins, cormorants and

At left: **A Bustard of the South African veldt.** *At right:* **Cape Gannets** *(top)* **and an Egyptian Vulture** *(below).*

other sea birds thrive here. The **Jackass Penguin** *(below and bottom left)* comes ashore to lay its greenish eggs in burrows dug into the guano-caked soil. Tons and tons of this phosphate-rich guano have been mined from offshore islands, destroying penguin habitats. Sharing these islands are several species of cormorants which, like penguins, swim underwater to catch fish and crustacea.

The **Ostrich** *(right, bottom right, and opposite)* is the world's largest living bird. The male may stand nine feet tall and weigh over 300 pounds! The Ostrich is adapted to life in arid environments. It is capable of withstanding high temperatures without dehydrating, and can run 40 mph across the open plains and deserts. Ostriches flock together in a breeding strategy that minimizes exposure to predators. Several females will deposit their eggs together in one nest to be tended by the sole male and the dominant female. One nest may contain a dozen eggs, each one weighing about two and one-half pounds. Ostriches are raised in South Africa for their feathers, leather and eggshells, and are run in races popular with bettors.

Bustards resemble small Ostriches and frequent similar grassland habitats for insects such as locusts and termites, and other small animals. **Kori Bustards** hunt singly or in pairs, swaying their heads while they walk. Bee-eaters often ride upon the bustard's back to eat insects disturbed into flight. **Heuglin's Bustards** are poor fliers, but run with great speed through thick savanna grasslands.

Helmeted Guinea Fowl *(opposite, top)* are stocky, turkey-like birds domesticated in the fourth century BC by the Romans. They are terrestrial birds, but can fly into trees to roost for the night. They eat insects and vegetable matter that are found in shrub and grassland habitats.

Swainson's Francolin *(top)* is a grouse-like bird able to exist in areas of dry savanna around the Kalahari Desert of southern Africa by eating wild melons and bulbs. The male crows from conspicuous perches at sunrise and sunset, and leads a family group of six or more.

The **Cattle Egret** *(below)* is one of the few cosmopolitan birds. Unassisted by man, Cattle Egrets from Africa have colonized the rest of the world in fewer than 50 years. They arrived in the New World in 1952. The reason for their success is a foraging behavior already adapted to take advantage of modern agricultural practices. Instead of following large African animals to feed on disturbed insects, they have learned to follow domestic animals and farm equipment.

The **Shoe-billed Stork** *(opposite, bottom)*, also known as the Whale-headed Stork, is limited to tropical east Africa. It is a unique wading bird with an enormous bill designed for catching African lungfish and other large aquatic prey. This species is the sole representative of its family, and little is known about its breeding habits except that it rattles and claps its gigantic bill during breeding displays. Its relationship to other stork-like birds is unclear. Suffice to say, it is an odd bird indeed!

With a curious growth on its colorful beak, a crimson spot on its breast, long, trailing legs and ponderous flight, the **Saddle-billed Stork** *(below)* is another unmistakable bird. Like the Shoe-billed Stork, the Saddle-billed Stork is found only in tropical Africa. It nests in large trees over water and forages in marshes and grasslands for crabs, shrimp, fish, frogs, mammals and young birds. It tosses its prey into the air to swallow it headfirst.

Marabou Storks *(opposite, bottom)* are scavengers of carrion. Their dagger-like bills ensure them their fair share when fighting with vultures and hyenas over a carcass. They will also eat frogs, fish and whatever else comes their way. The lack of feathers on their heads and throats is an adaptation to avoid bacterial buildup, as soiling with gore occurs when they feed inside rotting carcasses. With a wingspan of 11 feet, Marabou Storks take advantage of the thermal winds rising from African plains. From great heights they can spot other feeding flocks of storks and vultures.

Golden bristles adorn the heads of **Crowned Cranes** *(right and opposite top)*. They perform elaborate mating dances. As the wet season nears, much leaping in air, flapping of wings and many duets compose a display that bonds the pairs together for life.

Stanley's Cranes, named for the great African explorer who sought the legendary Dr Livingstone, are as stately in posture as they are muted in color. They are found in southern African fields and farmlands, as well as wetlands. Like other cranes, they pair for life.

Standing over five feet tall, the **Goliath Heron** is the largest of the herons. It spears fish with its giant bill in marshes of Africa and India. The Goliath Heron nests colonially in trees with members of its own — as well as other — species. **African Spoonbills** are shy and less social than most other water birds. When nesting, spoonbills segregate themselves in their nest trees from other herons and ibises. Spoonbills walk through shallow waters, sweeping their spatulate bills sideways and sifting mud for insects to eat.

Flamingoes *(right and opposite)* have unique bills, extremely long legs and necks, and use these appendages to full advantage. They feed with their necks bent and bills submerged in water, zig-zagging their heads from side to side as they filter insect larvae, shrimp and small mollusks from algae-rich waters. Flamingoes feed at large sheets of water, such as shallow coastal lagoons and salt pans in the interior of Africa. Highly gregarious, they also nest in colonies on mud platforms and rear a single chick. Flocks are especially beautiful in flight because of their white and scarlet plumage.

'*Ha Ha Ha Ah Ah Ah*,' the well-known, raucous cry of the **Hadedas Ibis** *(below)*, is heard throughout Africa. These birds commonly live in small flocks in plantations and in open grasslands near streams. They are solitary nesters, building a platform of sticks in trees or on telephone poles.

Hammerheaded Storks are considered sacred by many African tribes because they are thought to be harbingers of rain. One unique behavior of Hammerhead Storks is their architectural prowess. A breeding pair of Hammerheads will build a stick nest that may weigh a ton and measure five feet across. A cavity inside this fortress serves as the nest chamber. After breeding, the nest is abandoned and other species will take it over, Egyptian Geese nesting inside and Chanting Goshawks on top.

Egyptian Geese *(right and below)* use abandoned Hammerhead Stork nests in order to avoid snakes and other predators. Foul tasting, bad tempered and belligerent, it's a wonder this species was ever domesticated by the ancient Egyptians. Today, as in ancient times, Egyptian Geese invade grain fields and damage crops.

Red-billed Teals *(opposite, top)* are found in vast flocks, often with Yellow-billed Ducks. Teal are common in flooded fields and marshes, where they feed on aquatic plants, insects and small frogs. They build a nest of fine grasses and feather it with down from their breasts. **Yellow-billed Ducks** *(opposite, bottom)* are more wary than teal and fly high and fast when flushed. They are also common and gregarious, being found in large flocks in open water, marshes, lush grass and thick vegetation near estuaries, but are subject to losing habitats in drought-stricken Africa. They readily resort to the 'broken-wing' display to lead would-be predators away from their nests.

Crowned Plovers run along lake margins picking insects and crustacea from the mud. They also live in arid regions and grassland plains, where they hunt locusts in burnt-over areas. Flocks of plovers assemble before breeding to engage in communal dances.

An odd adaptation for a plover-like species, the large eyes of the **Spotted Thick-knee** are used for night hunting. The Thick-knee inhabits dry washes near temporary streams and arid plains near water. It lays three or four well-camouflaged eggs after scraping out a nest in the gravel.

One of only a few tool-using birds, **Egyptian Vultures** *(right)* are known to crack open Ostrich eggs by repeatedly dropping rocks on the shells. Their diet also includes carrion and human excrement, earning them the moniker 'Pharaoh's Chicken.' They perform a valuable service by cleaning up villages, making them less prone to disease.

The most attractive of scavengers, **White-headed Vultures** *(below and opposite, top)* have beautiful pastel-colored heads. They are carrion eaters but also are known to kill their own prey, suggesting a trait that they may have inherited from eagles. They breed in trees and on inaccessible cliffs, where they lay a single, large egg.

Secretary Birds *(opposite, bottom)* are unique birds of prey that hunt small mammals, birds and reptiles in the tall grass of the African savanna. When stalking or running through the grass, their long legs keep them out of reach of striking snakes. Secretary Birds are named for the plumes that look like quill pens stuck behind their ears.

A strikingly colored bird with rust-red, black and white plumage, the **Bateleur Eagle** *(opposite)* hunts the open grasslands and woods of the savanna for small mammals, birds and reptiles. *Bateleur* is a medieval French word for acrobat. Rolls, somersaults and teetering flight are identifying characteristics as this eagle rides the thermal winds rising from the grasslands. Its nest is a bulky affair of sticks, often close to roads and rivers. A single egg is laid and incubated by the female, who, in turn, is fed reptiles, birds, small, dead animals and termites by her mate.

The **African Fish Eagle** *(below)* belongs to the same genus as the Bald Eagle of North America and shows many similarities, including a white head. This common and widespread Fish Eagle is conspicuous and tame where it is not harassed. The Fish Eagle's favorite perch is a snag on a dead tree overlooking a slow moving river. When prey is spotted, it will swoop in and strike with one outstretched foot. Very broad wings enable the eagle to lift itself and a heavy fish from the water. Where prey is abundant, this eagle is found in high densities. It will establish and maintain hunting territories, and will steal fish from another of its species to obtain meals.

Chanting Goshawks *(right)*, named for their prolonged, musical piping, occur in dark and light colored species. The lighter species hunts in thorn bush and tall grass savanna, where their very long legs enable them to hunt effectively. They often will follow honey-badgers to catch lizards and large grasshoppers that the badgers scare

up. The darker species hunts doves and other arboreal birds, but also takes invertebrates off the ground.

White-faced Scops Owls *(opposite)* commonly live in pairs along dry watercourses in the dry Kalahari desert and surrounding savanna. Their adaptations to the desert include light coloration and a short tail for flying in treeless areas, where they hunt large insects and lizards. They nest atop abandoned hawk nests.

The black-faced **Namaqua Dove** *(right)* eats seeds in the dry savanna woodlands and old cultivated lands. The male's black mask and longer tail distinguish him from the drab female, but both sexes often raise and lower their tails upon alighting. Pairs incubate two cream-white eggs in a nest of twigs and rootlets, and in favorable conditions may breed year-round.

Knysna Touracos or **Loeries** *(below)* are beautiful birds found in evergreen forests in southern Africa. They are fairly large and run with great agility along the slender tree limbs. Touracos are hard to see in the dark, shadowy undergrowth, despite their bright red wings and blue and green feathers. Pigments in their plumage are unique among birds because they are water soluble. The colors in other bird plumages result from light refraction.

With a yellow face, crimson crest and wings and a loud, whistling call, the distinctive **Red-crested Touraco** is a bird of equatorial Africa, where it is found in tropical rain forests and cultivated orchards. Its diet consists of fruit, wild figs and some insects.

The **White-browed Coucals** are medium-sized birds that skulk in reed beds and dense thickets. Coucals are poor fliers, but their long, loose tails help balance them as they forage in tall grasses and branches that overhang marshes for vegetable matter and small animals such as frogs and mice.

Only four and one-half inches long, the **Pygmy Kingfisher** (*right*) and **Malachite Kingfisher** (*opposite*) appear similar, but the Pygmy Kingfisher lacks a crest. It is mainly found away from water, perching low and pouncing on ground insects such as crickets. The equally small Malachite Kingfisher hunts over water for frogs, fish and insects. Both species nest in burrows dug into cliff faces.

The **Giant Kingfisher** (*below*) is found south of the Sahara and is commonly distributed in appropriate habitats, from mountain streams to coastal lagoons. They usually nest in areas characterized by streamside trees, river and reservoir banks. The Giant Kingfisher eats mainly freshwater crabs, but it is considered a pest in areas where trout have been introduced.

Like kingfishers, bee-eaters are a colorful, long-billed species. Also like kingfishers, they nest colonially in tunnels dug into sandy cliffs. **Bee-eaters** *(opposite, top)* are adept at picking venomous bees out of the air and holding the stinging insects until the venom is pumped out. Some species are thought to be immune to the venom and swallow bees in midair. Other species specialize in eating lizards and dragonflies.

Swallow-tailed Bee-eaters *(opposite, bottom)* range from semi-desert to moist areas, but leave frost-prone regions in winter. Sometimes, groups will roost together for warmth, sitting on each other's backs three or four deep. They eat wasps, grasshoppers and will pluck insects from flowers.

Lilac-breasted Rollers *(right)* are colorful birds called 'blue jays' in South Africa, where they live singly or in pairs in arid lands. One interesting behavior is their attraction to grass fires. They have learned to hunt along the fire line for fleeing grasshoppers, locusts, caterpillars and even centipedes, scorpions and small birds. During the breeding season, rollers perform various aerial antics to impress their mates.

Yellow-billed Hornbills *(below)* are a common species in dry savannas, where they forage on the ground for flying insects, ants, termites, fruits, seeds and reptiles. They frequently visit villages and, if not harassed, become quite tame. The reproductive behavior of hornbills is unique among birds. The male plasters the female into the nest hole with guano and mud, leaving a crack for food and air to pass. The male then feeds his mate as she incubates the eggs. The strategy is to prevent predation of eggs and nestlings by bands of roving monkeys and tree snakes.

Looking like a cross between a kingfisher and a hornbill, **Red and Yellow Barbets** have a heavy bill bordered by bristles. They are ground-dwelling birds that eat mainly termites and ants. Like kingfishers, they nest in burrows dug into the earth, where they lay three dull-white eggs.

Paradise Flycatchers *(below)* are unmistakable with their elongated central tail feathers trailing in the wind. Rippling laughter, '*whee-wheeo-whit-whit*', is repeated as they sally in midair to catch flies. They prefer large trees near water for nesting, but also visit gardens and woods near human habitation. They may be approached closely while they are sitting on small, bowl-shaped nests. A red color variation of this species is found in deciduous and bamboo forests of Korea and China.

The **Cape Batis** is a flycatcher partial to moist upland forests of southern Africa. Incubating birds build a nest of rootlets and fibers covered with lichen in the fork of a branch. Two or three pinkish eggs are laid and hatch 17 days later. The chicks fledge after another 16 days. When the breeding season is completed, flocks gather to forage for insects.

With their characteristic white streaks, **Arrow-marked Babblers** *(right)* forage for insects in small bushes and thorn trees in the riverine forest, constantly 'babbling' among themselves. Calls may also be loud and crow-like. Babblers are generally dull colored, but this species is distinctively marked, and its turquoise eggs are especially beautiful.

Bulbuls belong to a large family of 120 species scattered across tropical Africa and Asia. **Red-eyed Bulbuls** *(opposite)* are found in

gardens and dry country near water holes and rivers, where they eat berries and insects. Shallow, cup-shaped nests of twigs, lined with fine grasses, are built in low thorn trees and bushes. Both sexes aggressively defend the two to four eggs.

Crimson-breasted Shrikes *(opposite, bottom)* are unmistakable in their gaudy plumage. They hop on the ground foraging for insects and nest in dry thorn trees. A shallow nest basin of rootlets, curled bark and fibers is constructed to hold two or three eggs. Shrikes impale their animal prey on thorns and barbed wire for later consumption, earning them the moniker 'butcherbirds.'

Another beautiful species is the **Bokmakierie Shrike** *(below)*, named for its unique call, which is repeated by mated pairs from conspicuous perches. It is a common garden species in southern Africa, nesting close to the ground around homesteads, where it hunts for chameleons, frogs and caterpillars.

Greater Double-collared Sunbirds *(opposite, top)* are feathered with iridescent greens, purples and brilliant reds. In the highlands of central Africa and at mid-elevations of South Africa, they haunt forest borders and sheltered valleys. They eat spiders and insects in addition to fruit juices and nectar. In arid environments, the flowers of aloe species are favored. Sunbirds suspend pendulous nests of grasses and hair from drooping vines.

The **Orange-breasted Sunbird** *(right)* is less gaudy than other members of this family. Noisy and active, it flits from one blossom to the next as it seeks insects, spiders and nectar. During winter

months, various sunbird species form feeding flocks. The territorial male repeats a characteristic call from his favorite perch.

The **Orange River White-Eye** *(opposite, top)* is one of several species and races of white-eyes found in Africa, a very large family in which over 60 species appear very similar. They are small, yellow-green birds, with a conspicuous white eye ring, which is probably used for interspecies recognition. Plumage differences can be attributed to humidity, diet (they eat fruit pulp, nectar and insects) and other unknown factors.

The smallest seed-eating bird on the African continent is the **Orange-breasted Waxbill** *(opposite, below)*, also known as the 'Goldbreast.' This tiny bird of the subSahara region inhabits reed beds, marshes, grasslands and dry, cultivated land, where it feeds on seeds, growing tips of vegetation and insects. It nests near the ground and often takes over old bird nests.

Blue Waxbills *(right)*, also known as 'Cordon-bleus' by cage bird fanciers, are another very small species. They are especially characteristic of the dry thorn scrub around human settlements in south and central Africa. Blue Waxbills do not actively defend their young, since any predator is too big and potentially dangerous for these tiny birds.

Vitelline Masked Weavers *(below)* are common in open woodlands of acacia or thorn trees, where they build two nests — one for roosting and one for incubating eggs. Large colonies of nests are woven from grasses and reeds and suspended from branch tips. Each

male has several mates. Each female lays a clutch of extraordinarily colored eggs, ranging from pure white or pink to blue-green, each one spotted, speckled or splotched!

The **Red-headed Weaver Finches** *(opposite)* fabricate elaborate nests at the tips of branches. The male fashions a frame of grass and twigs and weaves a round nest. He then adds a waterproof roof of broad leaves. The female works to shape the interior from within. Weaver Finches occur in localized populations in the dry savanna near water, preferring large trees in which to quietly creep along branches and look for insects, spiders and seeds.

Various races of **Red-billed Fire Finches** *(right)* are found throughout subSaharan Africa. These tame, tiny birds live in small groups around cultivated lands in scrub and near surface water. They peck seeds and jump after flying termites, and are frequently hunted by hawks and other predators.

Fearless and gregarious, **Superb Starlings** *(below)* are common residents of the dry savanna forest, often foraging in small groups on the ground. The starlings' diet of insects benefits farmers trying to grow grain crops. After courtships of jumping on the ground with drooping wings and outstretched necks, males build domed grass nests in trees or on cliffs, into which the female places four or five blue-green eggs. **Violet-backed Starlings** have shiny, metallic-colored plumage typical of African starlings. They live in dry thorn trees, feed on the ground, and form large flocks after breeding.

NORTH AMERICA

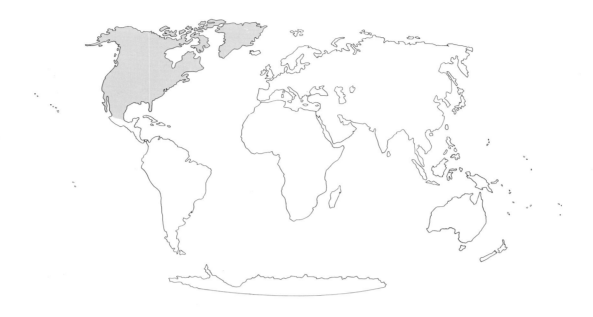

The continent of North America extends from the Arctic coast to the Gulf of Mexico and from the Atlantic to the Pacific Oceans. The great variety of North American vegetation and elevations provide habitats for more than 750 bird species. The vegetation zones of North America show patterns and are populated by avian assemblages similar to those of Eurasia. The arctic latitudes of the north are blanketed with low-lying tundra and marshes. The northern coasts and offshore islands are also habitat for myriad sea bird rookeries and serve as a land bridge for species exchange between Eurasia and North America.

Coniferous trees are characteristic of the far north. Stunted conifers cover most of northern Canada. The mountain ranges of western North America are covered in pines, firs and spruce, and the Northwest coast, receiving more than 200 inches of rain a year in some parts, is a temperate rain forest. California redwoods, hemlocks and Douglas firs of great age reach tremendous proportions where they are undisturbed. However, bird populations are relatively smaller than those in tropical rain forests.

The New World temperate zone is marked by the several mountain ranges that run north to south. In the West, the Sierra, Cascade and Rocky mountains block moisture from the Pacific Ocean from reaching the interior. Consequently, the Great Basin region and the midwest range is semi-arid, with pronounced seasonal changes. Originally covered with short and tall grass prairies, this area is comparable to the Eurasian steppes. Prairie Chickens and other grouse, sparrows and hawks are typical.

North America is drained by rivers that primarily run north to south. The greatest of these, the Mississippi, serves as a flyway that funnels birds from their Arctic breeding grounds in Canada to their wintering areas in the Gulf of Mexico. From the Mississippi River to the Eastern Seaboard, the hilly terrain is cloaked in deciduous forests. The southern regions are dry pine and hardwood forests, intergrading into subtropical hardwoods, and at the tip of Florida, tropical vegetation appears. The tremendous insect populations feed millions of songbirds, such as warblers and thrushes.

The deserts of the Southwest range well into Mexico and exhibit avifaunal affinities with Latin America. Many species, like Trogons, some hummingbirds and Gila Woodpeckers, are limited to this region. North American avifauna intergrades throughout Mexico with South American avifauna. The isthmus of Panama is a bridge between the two continents of the New World. At various periods, the rising seas flooded this narrow link and isolated the continents. At other times, receding waters exposed more land, thereby allowing poorly flying birds access in both directions. Tens of millions of birds migrate to South America in winter, when insects and fruit are

At left: A Snowy Egret. *At right:* A Ladder-backed Woodpecker.

unavailable in the north. Consequently, the accelerating loss of forests in South and Central America greatly affects wintering North American birds.

On remote northern lakes and tundra ponds, the cry of the **Arctic Loons** *(right)* is the sound of wilderness. Loons are primitive, fish-eating water birds. Fossils of similar species date back 70 million years. Loons construct reedy nests on floating vegetation. After hatching, the downy chicks ride on their parents' backs. In winter, Loons frequent bays and other saltwater environments near the shore.

Horned Grebes *(opposite, bottom)* are adapted to diving for aquatic insects. Because their legs are placed so far back, they dive with ease, but walk with difficulty on land. These duck-like birds with chicken-like beaks can slowly sink until completely submerged. **Eared Grebes** *(below)* are named for their ornamental breeding plumes. Like Loons, Grebes build nests of floating vegetation, and when the eggs hatch, the chicks ride on the backs of the parents. In the summer, Grebes breed on freshwater ponds, but in winter, they move to saltwater. The mating dance of the **Western Grebe** *(opposite, top left)* is a water ballet. Both partners rise up and skitter across the lake on webbed feet.

Yellow-throated **Double-crested Cormorants** *(opposite, top right)* prefer inland lakes and often nest alongside Egrets and Herons in trees. They construct nests of sticks and weeds, often stealing material from each other. When diving, they compress their wings against their bodies to remove trapped air, relying on layers of fat for insulation. Cormorants paddle with their feet while chasing prey, but after fishing, they must hold their wings 'spread eagle' to dry because they lack oil glands to waterproof their feathers.

The blue-throated **Brandt's Cormorants** *(below)* wag their heads and flip their wings to attract mates. After hatching, many chicks huddle together for warmth. These Cormorants nest, along with pelicans, on rocky islands in the north Pacific, especially off the coast of California.

With bills almost half as long as their bodies, **Brown Pelicans** *(opposite, top right)* appear clumsy on land, but they can fly with ease and dive expertly, plunging from great heights. Brown Pelicans are making a comeback from the brink of extinction. Pesticides affected their ability to lay eggshells of proper thickness. **White Pelicans** *(opposite, bottom)* frequently breed in large western lakes. Together, flocks herd fish into shallow water and scoop them up. In the breeding season, horny growths of unknown function develop atop their bills.

Sea bird colonies resemble a crowded, noisy apartment house. **Common Murres** *(right and opposite, top left)* crowd together on cliff ledges. Their green eggs are very pointed so they will roll only in a tight circle. Murres are the Arctic counterpart to the Antarctic Penguins. Like Penguins, Murres can swim underwater with their flipper-like wings. But unlike Penguins, they can also fly, though their short wings make it difficult for them to get airborne. To gain momentum for flight, Murres jump off cliff edges.

Tufted *(below, bottom left)* and **Horned Puffins** *(below, bottom right)* are colorful sea birds with parrot-like bills designed for catching fish. Their powerful beaks could easily crush a man's finger. Tufted Puffins dig burrows as far as 18 feet into the Earth. They stand outside their burrows like harlequin clowns. **Rhinoceros Auklets** *(opposite, bottom left)* and **Pigeon Guillemots** *(right)* nest amid the rocky rubble in burrows and crevices. **Western Gulls** *(opposite, top right)* are always on the lookout for eggs and chicks to eat. They will take those of other species as well as their own. All these sea birds nest on isolated islands free from predators and human disturbance.

At margins of quiet bays and estuaries, many species of shore birds feed in different manners. **Long-billed Curlews** *(below, center)* use their nine-inch, curved bills to catch worms and crabs in deep mud or water. **Marbled Godwits** wade knee-deep in water, their slightly upcurved bills probing for marine worms, clams and crabs.

In the shallows, **Black-necked Stilts** *(opposite, top left)* pick at the surface for brine shrimp and insects. Their long, red legs can carry them into deeper water than other shore birds can go. With their upturned bills, **American Avocets** *(opposite, bottom right)* filter organisms from the soupy mud. They hide their boldly patterned wings until they explode into flight. The sudden display alarms would-be predators. Both Stilts and Avocets nest side by side on marshy islands and brood their chicks under their wings.

138

Along the rocky coastline of the West Coast, **Black Oystercatchers** *(below)* use their red, chisel-like bills to jab and pry open shellfish so they can eat the rich meat. They are never quiet for long, piping out a warning '*kleep kleep kleep!*' Other species find food in sandy beaches. Seemingly forever in motion, diminutive **Sanderlings** *(opposite, bottom)* run after retreating waves. They quickly hunt in the sand before the next wave crashes.

Far out at sea, amid the constant waves, petite **Red Phalaropes** *(below, bottom left)* bob like corks. These marine shore birds pass along the coast in migration, but winter out of sight of land. They are reported to pick lice from whales lying at the surface. Sex roles are reversed in phalaropes. Females display the rich breeding dress and mate with several drab males, leaving each of them with a nest of eggs to tend.

Snowy Egrets *(right)* are elegant birds with black bills and legs, and golden yellow feet. Every spring, Egrets develop lacy plumes and, at the turn of the century, they often were killed for these fashionable accessories to ladies' hats. The National Audubon Society was formed to prevent the extinction of Egrets for frivolous fashion.

With their long white plumes, **Great Egrets** perform mating dances, but the feathers also serve another purpose. The birds crush filaments from the special feathers into a fine powder and apply the dust to remove fish slime from their plumage. Snowy and Great Egrets frequently hunt side by side in tidal marshes and nest together in tall trees. Great Egrets are distinguished by their larger size and yellow bills.

Black-crowned Night Herons *(right)* are medium-sized wading birds with short necks and stout bills. They become most active at sunset, when they leave their communal roosts to feed on fish, crabs and even other birds. They are distinguished by piercing, red eyes and a black crown capped by two white plumes. The brown-streaked immature juveniles resemble Bitterns.

American Bitterns *(opposite, bottom)* are well-camouflaged denizens of dense, reedy marshes. Colored in mute browns and blacks, they blend in superbly with their world. When confronted with a predator, they freeze with their bills pointing skyward, and seem to disappear from view.

Shy, secretive and rarely glimpsed, **Clapper Rails** *(opposite, top left)* are the voice of the marsh. Rather than flying to avoid disturbances, they compress their bodies and become as 'thin as a rail' as they run through the marsh. Eating snails and marine invertebrates, rails are trying to survive in spite of shoreline development and pollution.

American Coots *(opposite, top right)* are related to rails and are very much at home swimming or wading in shallow water because they have partially webbed feet. They are black, duck-like birds, with white frontal shields and bills. The orange-headed young are fed algae by the parents.

Tundra Swans *(below)* are huge, white water birds which graze on young grasses, grain and aquatic roots. By tipping up their rumps and extending their heads underwater, swans can access four feet of water. Swans form large flocks in winter and feed in uplands on spilled and excess corn and wheat. In the spring, pairs migrate to the far northern tundra, where they build a bulky nest of grasses on an island.

142

Eleven subspecies of **Canada Geese** *(opposite, bottom)* vary in size from three to 20 pounds. All appear very similar, with the typical white chin straps. Geese are increasingly common in reserves where hunting is prohibited. Modern technology has affected Canada Geese migration. Because mechanical corn pickers leave much grain in the fields, some subspecies abbreviate or forego migration altogether, their needs being met where they breed. Like swans, geese mate for life, and both parents vigorously protect the goslings until they can fly.

Emperor Geese *(below)* nest on the deltas of the great rivers that drain into the Bering Sea in the far northwestern regions of Alaska. In winter, they head to the rocky coasts bordering the Pacific Ocean, where they forage on eel grass, seaweed and algae. Along with **White-fronted Geese** *(opposite, top left)*, they provide the Eskimos with eggs and meat. 'Speckled bellies,' as they are also called, migrate from Alaska to the interior valleys of California and the Mississippi in the fall and winter, where they are much prized by hunters. Geese migrate from Alaska to the interior valleys of California and the Mississippi, where they are shot by hunters in the fall and winter.

Dabbling ducks are generally found in freshwater environments and eat seeds and vegetation found along pond margins. **Mallards** *(right)* are the most common duck in North America. The males' metallic green head is familiar to anyone who has ever visited a duck pond. Females are easily confused with **Gadwalls** *(opposite, top right)*, drab ducks of the marshes. Mallards interbreed with these related close-up species and domesticated European ducks to produce hybrids.

Pintails *(below)* are handsome white and brown ducks with long necks who, together with mallards, constitute the most frequently observed large wintering flocks. Pintails are one of the most abundant ducks of North America. Formerly known as 'baldpate,' owing to their white crown, **American Wigeons** *(opposite, top right)* utter a peculiar whistling quack while they feed on algae, seaweed and grains.

Shovelers are patterned like Mallards, except for their unique bills. They sieve animal and plant foods from lake bottoms and pond surfaces with these comb-like, spatulate bills. A depression in thick grass lined with down constitutes their nests.

Green-winged Teals *(right)* are the smallest ducks in North America, yet probably the fastest. These wary ducks can fly as fast as 160 mph and migrate about 125 miles a day.

Wood Ducks *(opposite, top left)* nest in tree hollows as high as 60 feet off the ground. Conservationists lure this most attractive duck by placing nest boxes in wooded swamps. The females incubate the eggs until they hatch and then call to their downy young, who step into the air and flutter helplessly to the water. Soon they can fly with great skill through a maze of trees.

Like the Wood Duck, beautiful **Hooded Mergansers** *(opposite, bottom)* nest in tree hollows in wooded areas, but they have narrow, serrated bills for catching fish in streams. The females are dull colored to avoid detection.

146

California Condors are the largest birds in North America. With a wingspread spanning over 10 feet, Condors are masters of flight; they can glide on the wind for hours, covering hundreds of miles. Condors are also one of the most seriously endangered species in the world. Laying only one egg every other year, Condors breed very slowly, so that over the years, breeding Condors have not been able to replace the birds lost to age, guns and poison. Scientists are now trying to breed the last 28 birds in captivity, hoping to preserve the species from extinction.

A massive yellow beak, white head and tail, and dark brown body mark adult **Bald Eagles** *(below and opposite)*, America's symbol of freedom. Bald Eagles eat fish found in lakes and rivers, and along seacoasts. Alaska supports the largest Eagle population. Elsewhere, they are classified as a threatened or endangered species. Eagles mate for life and return to the same nest sites, usually in tall trees. Each spring, pairs renew their bonds with spectacular mating flights. Birds dive at each other, lock talons and tumble in flight. Two young are usually reared each year. Juveniles remain mottled brown until their fourth year, when they molt into the adult plumage. Bald Eagles sometimes rob other birds, as well as scavenge dead and dying fish. This behavior led Benjamin Franklin to suggest they that perhaps they were inappropriate as a mascot for a new nation.

Golden Eagles *(right)* are the 'most powerful birds of North America. They can kill prey five times their own weight, but mainly

eat rabbits and ground squirrels. They even eat carrion when live prey is scarce. Eagles are completely protected by law, but they are still occasionally shot by sheep ranchers, who claim they kill lambs. Eagle territories must be at least thirty square miles to provide enough food to support breeding efforts. Golden Eagle nests, called eyries, are stick nests built on high cliff ledges. Generations of eagles nest in them. Young eagles learn to fly on strong mountain winds and become masterful fliers.

With long, narrow wings spanning six feet, **Ospreys** *(right and opposite, top)* hover up to 100 feet over the water while scanning for fish. When prey is sighted, the bird folds its wings and dives feet first into the water. Ospreys have roughened feet and front toes that rotate to hold squirming fish. These birds are able to carry a three-lb fish — the average weight of the birds themselves! Each year, pairs perform the mating ritual of the 'fish flight.' After spectacular dives and swoops, the males present the females with a fish to demonstrate that they are good providers; later they must catch about six lb of fish each day to feed their growing chicks.

Falcons are narrow-winged Hawks of open country. Unmatched for speed and skill, black-hooded **Peregrine Falcons** *(below)* reach almost 200 mph in hunting dives, enabling them to slay even duck-sized birds through in-flight impact. Pesticides have reduced Peregrine Falcon numbers, but in recent years, populations are recovering and returning to nest on skyscrapers and bridges in the East and high mountains or islands in the West.

The smallest Falcon is also the most colorful. **Kestrels** *(opposite, bottom)* are orange-brown and slate-gray. They are commonly seen

hovering over a spot in the field or sitting on wires intently watching the ground for the movement of any insect, mouse or small bird.

Red-tailed Hawks (below) are the most common birds of prey in North America. A very adaptive species, they are found in farmlands, marshes, mountains and deserts across America. Redtails eat rodents that are spied while they soar up to one-half mile away. Their piercing scream is frequently imitated by Jays. **Rough-legged Hawks** are Eagle-like, with a wingspan approaching five feet. Marked by a white rump and black belly band, Rough-legged Hawks nest on cliffs and hunt rabbits in the Arctic tundra. **Ferruginous Hawks** (opposite, bottom) are also large, open country birds. In the Great Plains region, Ferruginous Hawks hunt jack rabbits and nest on low, isolated juniper trees.

Great Horned Owls (right and opposite top) are fearless and strong, killing raccoons, skunks and rabbits. By day, they roost in dense trees to avoid detection by crows and jays, which will attack and harass them until they leave the area. Owls avoid competing with hawks by hunting at night. Using acute hearing and sight, they can locate live prey in total darkness. Their night vision is more than thirty times greater than that of humans. Like humans, owls have forward-facing eyes that give them a high degree of binocular vision. Unlike humans, they can rotate their heads to look completely behind themselves.

Not all owls are night hunters. **Burrowing Owls** *(opposite)* can be found during the day, standing atop abandoned ground-squirrel holes. With long legs, these ground-dwelling owls hunt for beetles in open fields. They can see well in bright light because the pupils in their yellow irises contract to pinpoints.

The **Screech Owl's** *(right)* name is really a misnomer, because its characteristic wailing cry is not at all screechlike. A bird of woodland groves and forests, it is found throughout North America. Like hawks, owls kill with their talons and tear food apart with their hooked beaks. Owl pellets — bundles of regurgitated fur and bone — litter the forest floor beneath nests. Farmers are happy because the owls keep the mice population in check.

Three species of Ptarmigan are found in tundra areas where willow thickets abound. The **Willow Ptarmigan's** *(below, bottom right)* diet and plumage change with the seasons. In the spring, it eats buds and molts into gray and brown plumage. In the brief summer, insects and russet plumage are the style. Snow-white plumage and berries mark the fall and winter. Ptarmigans are feathered all the way to their toes. This not only keeps them warm, but also acts as 'snowshoes.' **White-tailed Ptarmigans** are found on mountain slopes where grasses and berry bushes grow. **Rock Ptarmigans** *(below)* range in high altitude zones, from Alaska into the southern Rocky Mountains.

Sage Grouse *(below, center right)* have elaborate displays. In the western sagebrush, several males perform the ritualized mating dance at staging grounds called leks. Males inflate hidden throat pouches and stick out their chests. Then, with feathers erect and orange

pouches exposed, they strut and stomp their feet. Females gather nearby and mate with the vigorous dancers.

Sharp-tailed Grouse *(below)* are nondescript inhabitants of the western brush lands, where they eat grasshoppers, crickets, acorns and waste seeds from agricultural land. Their mating dance has inspired elements of Indian dances — rhythmically stamping feet and bowed, prominently feathered heads.

'Fool hen' is the vernacular name for the **Spruce Grouse** *(opposite, top)*. In general, grouse are naturally tame, but their behavior becomes wary with the experience of being hunted. They eat spruce buds and needles, insects and mushrooms in the northern coniferous forests. Black-bellied males spread out a white collar of feathers to expose their red air sacs in a breeding display. Females, dappled in brown plumage, sit inconspicuously on mossy nests.

As their name implies, **Prairie Chickens** *(right)* are grassland birds. The Lesser Prairie Chicken is a threatened species because of the extent of land under plow. The finely barred Greater Prairie Chicken is likewise endangered. Both species survive in remnants of the tall and short grass prairies of the Midwest.

Wild Turkeys *(opposite, bottom)* were once so common and characteristic of the continent that Benjamin Franklin recommended them as the national bird. As the forests were logged, the turkey's

range diminished. They need tracts of deciduous woods to provide acorns and other seeds. Today, these birds have been reintroduced to areas within their former range and appear to be flourishing. Male gobblers form a harem of several females. Males stand almost four feet tall, spreading their tails and inflating their chests during breeding displays. Ever alert for danger, they herd their females until mating is over. The females care for the young throughout the winter, and several broods may join a common flock.

Doves are generally ground-feeding game birds selecting seeds, grain and fallen fruit, buds, young grasses and insects. **White-winged Doves** are abundant in brush lands of the Southwest. They arrive from Mexico in the early spring to nest in large colonies in mesquite scrub.

Mourning Doves *(right)* nest throughout North America and are the most hunted game bird. More than 30 million are bagged each year! Their swift, direct flight provides an ample challenge. Doves are dependent on farmlands for food and on brushy trees for nesting. The parents feed the young a milky substance produced from the foods they eat.

The **Greater Roadrunner** *(below and opposite)* is a ground cuckoo, also known as the 'chaparral cock' for the habitat it prefers. A poor flier, this bird is fast on its feet, quick enough to catch lizards and snakes. The Roadrunner warms itself by exposing the skin of its back to the early morning sun.

Rock Wrens *(opposite, top right)* inhabit the dry mountains of the West. Dressed in drab plumage, they flit about rocky crevices searching for spiders and moths. Their nests are hidden in rocky niches, but the entrances are paved with rock chips. The largest wrens in North America, **Cactus Wrens** *(below)*, are birds of the arid West, where they place dome-shaped nests in the arms of prickly cactuses.

Carolina Wrens *(right)* are the most brightly colored wrens. They inhabit the tangled undergrowth of the Southeast, and in recent years have expanded their range into the Northeast. In spring, their loud, cheerful song bursts forth from their nests in the underbrush. In the winter, they survive by visiting suet feeders.

Dippers *(opposite, top left)* are like giant, plump wrens with short, stubby tails. On land, they constantly 'bob' as if to keep warm, but they do something a wren would never do! Dippers dive into cold, mountain streams and use their wings to travel along the bottom and seek aquatic insect larvae.

Nesting in shrubs and fruit trees, **Robins** *(opposite, below)* are one of the most familiar birds of North America. Each evening in suburbs across the land, a chorus may be heard. During the day, these thrushes are seen periodically running and listening, then tugging and pulling worms from lawns. Albino robins periodically occur. **Wood Thrushes** are the forest counterpart to robins. They have a spotted breast and a fine, melodious song that they sing from the understory of deciduous forests in the Northeast.

160

Brown Thrashers *(right)* are medium-sized, long-tailed birds with great powers of mimicry. Thrashers sing a variety of phrases from a conspicuous perch to proclaim their territory.

Cardinals *(below)* have stout beaks for cracking tough seeds and opening pine cones. Cardinals are a common sight in backyards in the East. In fact, seven states have chosen them as their state bird. During this century, they have expanded their range northward and westward.

Wine-colored **House Finches** are common urban birds readily adapting to manmade environments. They were introduced to the East Coast in the 1940s and rapidly spread. **Goldfinches** *(opposite, bottom)* are common birds at feeders and in weedy fields. They eat the seeds of many plants, but prefer thistles above all else. Males are recognized by their mustard-yellow bodies and black foreheads, females by their dull green color.

Chestnut-backed Chickadees *(opposite, top)* are acrobatic insectivores that frequent brushy areas, woods and streamside vegetation. They hang upside-down or flit nervously about, investigating a new food source or anyone imitating their distinctive whistled call. Chickadees will mob small owls, scolding them into retreat. This mobbing behavior is also displayed by smaller birds.

Colorful and very active, warblers are the butterflies of the bird world. During the spring, these gaily feathered bundles of energy flit among the treetops eating insects. The **Yellow-rumped Warbler** *(right)* and **Yellowthroat** *(below, center)* are common all year in North America. Most other warbler species, such as the ground-nesting **Ovenbird** *(below, bottom left)* and **Wilson's Warbler** *(below, bottom right)*, migrate to Central and South America during the winter and return in the spring. They are insectivores and consume vast quantities of caterpillars and other harmful insects, but pesticide pollution and deforestation are affecting their numbers.

The **Red-eyed Vireo** *(opposite top)* is a rather sluggish (by warbler standards) insect eater that migrates to North America to breed. Because it nests at treetop level, the Red-eyed Vireo may be one of the most common — but little seen — members of the forest bird community.

By rapping on wood and listening to the sound, **Downy Woodpeckers** *(opposite, bottom left)* locate burrowing wood beetles and termites. Using sharp, chisel-like bills and shock-absorbing skulls, woodpeckers excavate their prey and nest holes each year.

Yellow-bellied Sapsuckers *(opposite, bottom right)* drill small pits into the bark of trees. Ants and other insects are attracted to the sweet, flowing sap. The sapsucker then returns to the sap that has collected in pools and laps up the insects and the nutritious liquid.

Gila Woodpeckers *(opposite, bottom)* are desert birds that fashion their homes out of giant saquaro cactuses. The woodpeckers excavate holes, which dry hard and gourd-like, in the fleshy plant. The nests serve the Gila Woodpeckers for several generations before being abandoned to other birds.

Common Nighthawks *(opposite, top right)* are nocturnal insect eaters that fly over fields and small cities 'hawking' moths. They are barely noticeable as they roost on tree limbs during the day. They also nest on rooftops, and may be heard overhead on summer evenings giving a characteristic '*peent.*'

One of the most colorful North American breeding birds, **Scarlet Tanagers** *(below)* are brilliantly hued, thrush-sized forest dwellers with black wings and tails set off by vibrant scarlet bodies. **Western Tanagers** *(opposite, top left)* rival the eastern species with their lemon yellow bodies and red heads. Tanagers are highly migratory and spend the winter in Latin America eating insects and fruit.

Loggerhead Shrikes *(right)* are medium-sized, masked birds with strong feet and hooked bills. They hunt from exposed perches in open fields. Also known as 'butcherbirds,' they impale insects and small animals on barbed wire to eat at their leisure.

Crested birds with tawny plumage, **Cedar Waxwings** *(below)* sing trilling notes from atop fruit trees. Flocks may boldly descend on suburban ornamental shrubs to consume the berries. Their name is derived from the red droplets on their wingtips.

Iridescent green and purple plumage with white eyes distinguish **Brewer's Blackbirds** *(opposite, bottom)*. In the West, they inhabit open areas, especially farmlands, city parks and pastures. **Redwing Blackbirds** *(opposite, top right)* are marsh and wetland inhabitants found all across the continent. Both blackbird species are gregarious and form large flocks in winter.

Orioles are related to blackbirds and share their characteristic sharply pointed bills. Black hoods, masks and wings contrast with orange or yellow plumage. The **Northern Oriole** *(opposite, top left)* is the most common species seen all across the continent in summer. Formerly known as the Baltimore Oriole, this species was grouped with the western Bullock's Oriole because they interbreed at the margins of their respective ranges.

Also related to blackbirds, **Western Meadowlarks** *(right)* are bold songsters of the fields. Perched atop their favorite post, they unleash a melodious series of whistles and flute-like notes. These are ground-foraging birds that inhabit grassland areas.

168

Magpies, crows and jays are bold, intelligent and curious. Their raucous cries and conspicuous presence make them a familiar sight. **Yellow-billed Magpies** *(below, right)* are found only in the agricultural valleys of California, where they build large, stick nests in the centers of oaks and defend them against all comers like their cousins, the far-ranging **Common Magpie**. **American Crows** *(opposite, bottom)* are usually seen in flocks overhead or feeding in fields. When breeding season comes, they are extremely secretive and unusually silent. **Steller's Jays** *(opposite, top left)* are common in coniferous forests of the West. **Scrub Jays** *(opposite, top right)* inhabit chaparral and bushy areas of the West Coast and central Florida. Both jays are extremely territorial and will fight their own reflections in windows and mirrors.

Song Sparrows *(below)* are the most adaptable and widespread species of sparrow. Generally, they prefer bushy areas, where they forage for seeds and insects and sing their melodic song from a conspicuous perch.

Brown Towhees *(right)* are twice the size of average sparrows. They are found in the chaparral of California, where they forage on the ground. Towhees are territorial and live in pairs.

SOUTH AMERICA

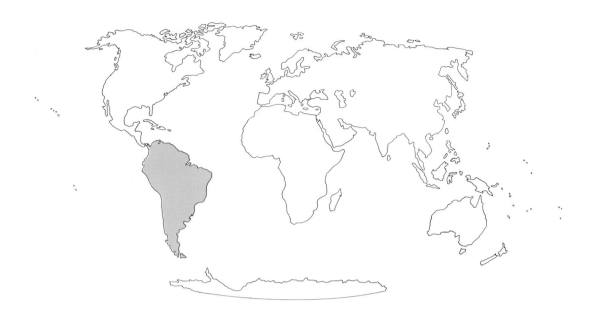

More than 3000 species of birds are indigenous to the continent of South America. The isolation and position of South America are the primary reasons for this assemblage of birds, richer by far than that found on any other continent. South America has been centered on the equator for many millions of years and the tropical rain forest that covers the bulk of the land drained by the Amazon, the greatest river of all, is ancient. During periods of glaciation, when ice covered much of North America, South America remained warm and wet. Thus, for a long period of time, the forests, and the birds that dwell within, have had a stable environment in which to evolve. Over the millennia, new species derived from more ancient, ancestral ones dispersed, some moving north across the Central American land bridge to colonize North America after the ice ages had passed.

The country of Colombia lies at the crossroads of the two continents. It alone hosts more than 2300 species because it has mountains and extensive rain forests. The rain forest of the Amazon basin covers two million square miles and supports more than 600 species of birds, almost as many as in all of North America! A region of rain and sun, this very productive environment is the home of wildly colorful birds such as toucans, tanagers and troupals. In the bright sunlight of the forest canopy, such colors are necessary in order for the birds to be visible to each other. In the dank, dark understory, muted shades are needed to avoid detection by predators. The rain forest is, however, very vulnerable, and a tragedy is in the making as a tremendous amount of acreage is cut down each day to harvest forest products and to clear land for agriculture. This rich, ancient environment cannot be replaced, and the species that dwell there are being left homeless, so that hundreds of bird species will eventually cease to exist.

The land of South America varies greatly in topography. The Andes Mountains run like a massive spine down the west coast of the continent. This land of ice and snow reaches from the equator to the subAntarctic region, including a wide array of habitats in its vertical relief. In the southern, more temperate regions, the Andes Mountains block moisture from reaching the interior. High altitude grasslands, called the *altoplano*, and the lowland *pampas* cover the tapering tip of the continent. Birds similar to those of the African savanna occur here.

North American songbirds migrate to the forests of Central and South America in the winter by crossing the Gulf of Mexico or migrating down the coast. In a very real sense, they are residents, because they spend most of the year here and are only visitors to the north. That is why deforestation and uncontrolled use of pesticides is

At left: **A Red and Green Macaw of South America.** *At right:* **A Purple Gallinule (top) and a Rufous Hummingbird (bottom).**

a concern for both North and South America. Shore birds breed in the arctic winter in the lower *pampas*, and birds of prey winter in the Mexican and South American woodlands. So, with a host of migrants and a rich population of indigenous birds, South America is truly the bird continent of the world.

Magellanic Penguins *(right)* live on the southern tip of South America. Huge colonies, numbering more than one million, are established in the deserts along the coast of Argentina. Here, penguins dig burrows in the dry earth and lay a pair of eggs. Composed of loud braying and fights, the ruckus in the colony continues for about six months until the adults and young return to the sea. Cold Antarctic currents promote food production in the southern waters. Tongues of fertile waters extend up the western coast, supporting millions of cormorants, pelicans and terns.

Mustachioed and with red mouths and slate-gray plumage, **Inca Terns** *(opposite)* are dapper birds of the west coast of South America. Fishing in the cold water currents off Peru, they are the only species of terns to nest in cliff holes.

Black-bellied Tree Ducks *(below)*, also known as Red-billed Whistling Ducks, nest in trees along stream margins from south Texas to northern Argentina. They are nocturnal ducks, feeding in shallow waters and cornfields. These long-legged ducks can fly among wooded swamps and land in trees with ease. A high-pitched whistle is characteristic of these ducks and the related **Fulvous Tree Ducks**, which thrive throughout the warmer areas of this bioregion.

174

The **Muscovy Duck** has been domesticated from a wild species found in Central and South American swamps. Its naked skin is covered with fleshy knobs and wattles.

Lesser Magellanic Geese *(right)* are found in two populations: one on the southern coast, including the Falkland Islands, and one in the Andes Mountains. Some migration in winter is typical. Their distinctive barring is highly variable. They are related to the Shelducks and Cape Barren Geese of Australia and, like them, graze upland with sheep.

Wood Storks *(below and opposite, top)* are common in the tropics from Florida south through Mexico and into South America. They breed in the dry season when ponds evaporate, making fishing easier, and nest in colonies in islands of trees with Roseate Spoonbills and other waders. Black and white Wood Storks are often seen soaring in large flocks high above the marshes.

Looking like something from Alice in Wonderland, **Roseate Spoonbills** *(opposite, bottom)* use their spatulate bills to sift organisms from the watery ooze of estuaries and rivers. They feed with ibises and herons, each species using their peculiar bills to feed on different prey, thereby avoiding competition with one another. They nest together in loose colonies.

Boat-billed Herons (*opposite, top left*) have amazingly wide bills that they use to capture frogs at night and resonate their booming calls. They are found in thick vegetation overhanging slow, tropical streams and swamps. Looking like Black-crowned Night Herons, they share their habit of hunting after dark. It is then that their broad beaks come into play when they capture food by touch.

Scarlet Ibises (*below*) live in dense mangrove swamps bordering the coasts of northern South America. With their down-curved beaks, they probe the soft mud for crabs, frogs, fish and insects. Flocks of these birds in flight are a spectacular sight along the coast.

Chilean Flamingoes (*right*) occur from Peru south to Chile. Flamingoes submerge their bills and filter crustacea from shallow waters. They nest in large colonies on alkaline lakes and salt lagoons, constructing columnar mud nests in which single eggs are incubated. The young are downy-white, becoming pink as the color from their food is transferred.

Black Vultures (*opposite, top right*) are a ubiquitous presence around village dumps, where they scavenge offal or strip meat from a dead leatherback sea turtle, as pictured here on the coast of Costa Rica. Black Vultures often are seen with **Turkey Vultures** (*opposite, bottom*), and appear to depend on them to locate carrion by smell. The more aggressive birds descend and drive off the Turkey Vultures. Turkey Vultures have such keen senses of sight and smell that they can locate dead mice on the forest floor.

These pages: **Black Vultures with the carcass of a leatherback sea turtle.**

The **King Vulture** *(right)* is the most ornately colored vulture in the world. Found from Mexico south to Argentina, it is nevertheless a scarce bird found only in remote areas. These vultures all have naked heads so that feathers are not soiled with gore when feeding on rotten carcasses.

The **Crested Caracara** *(below)* is the national bird of Mexico and adorns its currency. This long-legged bird of prey generally hunts on foot, walking plowed fields and turning over earth clods to look for insects, snakes, lizards and mammals. Part predator and part scavenger, the Crested Caracara will also join Black Vultures in a carrion feast, but it will harass the large birds, forcing them to disgorge their prey. Only its colorful face is free of feathers.

The **Andean Cock of the Rock** *(opposite, top)* is a uniquely plumaged bird of the lower levels of the tropical forests. The males engage in communal displays on cleared areas of the forest floor. Each male postures and positions himself, relative to females present, to display his peculiarly shaped crest. The female chooses a mate and builds a shelf-like nest of mud, roots and saliva on a cliff face.

Flocks of **Keel-billed Toucans** *(opposite, bottom)*, with their long, hollow-cored beaks, move through the upper canopy of the rain forest eating fruit and bird eggs. Toucans are represented by 43 species, each with a different sized beak. The beak functions as a 'flag' for communication and a tool for courtship.

Quintessentially tropical, **Military** *(opposite, top left)*, **Scarlet** and **Hyacinth Macaws** *(opposite, top right)* are very large parrots of the New World. They inhabit the lowland rain forests from tropical Mexico to Argentina. Macaws live up to 70 years and are monogamous. Macaws are noted for their beautiful plumage, colorful, naked faces, harsh voices and powerful beaks.

Conures, also known as American parakeets, are small parrots with long, pointed tails. **Orange-fronted Conures** *(below right)* are found throughout the range of dry woodland termites. The relationship between these two species is exhibited by other parrots of Australia. Conures dig out nests in earthen termite mounds found scattered throughout the dry woodlands. **Golden Conures** *(opposite, bottom)* are found only in a small section of Brazil near the mouth of the Amazon River. An uncommon bird in rain forests, Golden Conures are treetop species that feed on fruit and nectar.

Wattled Curassows *(below, bottom left)* are turkey-like birds that do much of their foraging on the ground, feeding on vegetable matter such as fruit. These large birds are hunted as food and have become scarce near villages. They build a platform of sticks in low trees and lay several eggs.

White-headed Piping Guans *(right)* are similar to curassows but are smaller, chicken-sized birds. They are also more arboreal and are able to evade hunters. Guans are found in heavily wooded areas but are becoming scarce throughout their ranges.

Giant Peruvian Coots *(below)* occur in high altitude lakes in the Andes Mountains. Like other species of coots, they eat algae and insects.

Hummingbirds (*opposite, top and bottom*) are jeweled diadems of the New World forests and gardens. Evocative names like spangled coquette, red-throated sapphire, and white-tailed emerald capture the radiance of their iridescent plumage. These miniatures, the smallest of birds, feed on nectar, small insects and flower pollen. Hummingbirds hover like helicopters by beating their wings up to 80 times a second and rotating the wings through 180 degrees. Hundreds of species occur in Central and South America.

Troupials (*below, right*) are large yellow and black orioles that nest in groups in the tropical woodlands of Colombia and Venezuela. They eat a diet of fruit, insects and lizards and sing a loud, musical song.

Tropical Kingbirds (*below, bottom left*) are common on wires across the agricultural lands of Central and South America. They hunt insects, catching them in midair. Kingbirds are territorial and will pursue birds of prey and crows if they venture too close. Tropical Kingbirds fly north in the fall, visiting North America in small numbers.

Brazilian Cardinals (*below*) and **Venezuelan Cardinals** (*right*) are finches of the New World tropics found in gardens and forest borders, where they eat seeds and insects. With a waxy red head, Brazilian Cardinals are unmistakable, especially in Hawaii, where they have been introduced.

Resplendent Quetzals have been called the most beautiful birds in the world. Surely they are in contention, with their two-foot tails and metallic green and red plumage. They are found in the cloud forests in the mountains of Central America, where they nest in

187

rotting trees. They dig holes into the cores of these trees and lay several eggs in a nest of wood pulp. Often, high winds blow down the water-logged nest sites. The quetzal was worshiped by the ancient Mayas. It is the national symbol of Guatemala and is pictured on its currency.

Trumpeters *(right and opposite)* are hump-backed, rail-like birds that inhabit the rain forests of the Amazon basin. Their black, velvety plumage with iridescent highlights blends into the shadowy undergrowth, yet their loud, trumpeting voices make their presence known during courtship. When pursued, they run quickly and are a favorite target of Indian hunters, who imitate the booming call to bring them into shooting range.

Crested Seriemas *(below)* are grassland birds that hunt reptiles and insects in the *pampas* of South America. Crested Seriemas are shy and prefer to escape by running, flying short distances only when hard pressed. They find low branches to roost for the night and to nest. They are similar to the African Secretary Bird, both species having evolved in grassland habitats.

The **Chilean Tinamou** is a large, pheasant-like bird of the open thorny, scrub and grasslands, including grain fields of the Andes Mountains. It is related to the running, flightless birds, but can fly if hard pressed. These birds, including the introduced population on Easter Island, are hunted for meat. The male tends some of the most richly marked and glossy eggs in the bird world. The precocious chicks can run when they hatch and fly when half grown.

INDEX

Below: **Adelie Penguins of Antarctica.** ***Overleaf:*** **The Northern Bald Ibis of Eurasia.**